Ireland

and the
Classical
World

Philip Freeman

T0340677

UNIVERSITY OF TEXAS PRESS

AUSTIN

This book has been supported by an endowment dedicated to classics and the ancient world, funded by grants from the National Endowment for the Humanities, the Gladys Krieble Delmas Foundation, the James R. Dougherty, Jr. Foundation, and the Rachael and Ben Vaughan Foundation, and by gifts from Mark and Jo Ann Finley, Lucy Shoe Meritt, Anne Byrd Nalle, and other individual donors.

Requests for permission to reproduce material from this work should be sent to Permissions, University of Texas Press, P.O. Box 7819, Austin, TX 78713-7819.

⊗ The paper used in this book meets the minimum requirements of ANSI/NISO Z39.48-1992 (R1997) (Permanence of Paper).

LIBRARY OF CONGRESS CATALOGING-IN-PUBLICATION DATA

Freeman, Philip, 1961–
  Ireland and the classical world / by Philip Freeman.— 1st ed.
    p.   cm.
  Includes bibliographical references and index.
  ISBN 0-292-72518-3 (alk. paper)
    1. Ireland—History—To 1172—Sources.   2. Irish language—Foreign elements—Latin.   3. Latin language—Influence on Irish.
  4. Ireland—Relations—Greece.   5. Greece—Relations—Ireland
  6. Ireland—Antiquities, Roman.   7. Ireland—Relations—Rome.
  8. Rome—Relations—Ireland.   9. Romans—Ireland—History.
  10. Civilization, Classical.   I. Title.
  DA931 .F74   2000
  303.48′23615038—dc21   00-027762

Ireland and the Classical World

For Alison

Contents

List of Illustrations

FIGURES

TABLES

Introduction

Toward the end of the first century of our era, the Roman general Agricola stood on the shore of southern Scotland gazing a few miles across the Irish Sea at the rolling green hills of an island he knew to be rich in agricultural and mineral wealth. However, he did not invade Ireland, nor did the legions of Rome ever raise their banners over the fertile plains of Ulster or the rocky pastures of Connemara. Ireland remained beyond the political frontiers of Rome during the centuries when the empire controlled nearby Britain and Gaul; nevertheless, there was steady contact between Ireland and the classical world. Literary and archaeological evidence show that Ireland was known to the Greeks and Romans for hundreds of years, and that Mediterranean goods, and even travelers, found their way to Ireland, while the Irish at least occasionally visited, traded, and raided in Roman lands.

This book, the first ever written on relations between Ireland and the classical world, is an interdisciplinary study of all evidence linking early Ireland to the civilized lands of the Mediterranean during antiquity. The primary focus is on the literary evidence of Greek and Latin texts—that is, what the classical authors said about Ireland—but archaeological, linguistic, and other pieces of the complex puzzle are explored as well. Chapter One begins with a brief survey of archaeological evidence for contact between Ireland and the Mediterranean world. Chapter Two examines the linguistic evidence for Hiberno-Roman relations, including early Irish borrowing of Latin words and possible Roman inspiration for the Irish Ogam alphabet. Chapter Three goes beyond the evidence of archaeology and language to the classical accounts of Ireland in ancient literature. This, the main body of the book, is a comprehensive survey of every word the ancient Greek and Roman authors wrote about Ireland that survives, from claims of Irish cannibalism and exploding cattle to detailed geographical descriptions of the island's rivers and towns.

The boundaries of the material studied in this book stretch back as far as the earliest classical references to Ireland, perhaps dating to the fifth century B.C. The closing date of the study is more arbitrary in many ways, as the transition from classical times to the early medieval period in Ireland and western Europe in general is somewhat fluid. I have chosen the traditional date of the arrival of St. Patrick (A.D. 432) as a terminus, both because the classical world of the western Roman empire had collapsed by this date and because the establishment of Christianity marked a fundamental change from ancient to medieval Irish history. This is not to say that pre-Christian Irish culture disappeared with the introduction of the new religion—far from it. But after St. Patrick, Christianity opened Ireland to the influence of the Mediterranean world to a degree far greater than in the previous centuries of limited contact.

This book is written for everyone interested in the history of Ireland during ancient times, whether scholar or enthusiast. Accordingly, I have supplied original-language texts and detailed references to classical and secondary literature for those with a scholarly inclination, as well as explanations of obscure terms and translations of all Greek, Latin, and Irish words and passages for the general reader. In a few instances, a limited knowledge of the Greek alphabet is helpful; thus a chart with English equivalents is included (see Appendix 1). All the translations are my own and are literal rather than literary, preserving as closely as possible the original sense, sound, and sometimes the confusing ambiguities of the texts.[1] Forms in italics indicate transliterations of the original-language text (e.g., *Hibernia*); otherwise, standard modern forms are commonly used (e.g., "Ireland"). To avoid unnecessarily distorting the original words of the ancient authors, no attempt has been made to Latinize Greek names for Ireland or its tribes, towns, and rivers in the translations of their words (thus *Iwernia* instead of *Ivernia*, and *Woluntioi* rather than *Voluntii*).

As in any study of this kind, my work builds on the labor of many scholars who have preceded me, although earlier studies of the relations between

Ireland and classical civilization are not numerous. Examinations of the references to Ireland and the Irish in classical literature began as early as the second decade of the twentieth century with Francis Haverfield, who also surveyed Roman artifacts unearthed in Ireland, and Eoin MacNeill.[2] However, the sections on Greek and Roman authors from James Kenney's first volume on the sources for early Irish history have been by far the most thorough and helpful for scholars and general readers alike.[3] Kenney's pioneering work collecting the classical references to Ireland was the foundation of my research. Other more recent studies have also contributed to our understanding of the ancient literary evidence, including work by J. F. Killeen, J. J. Tierney, and Albert Rivet and Colin Smith.[4] For the study of archaeological evidence of Mediterranean contacts with Ireland, Seán Ó Ríordáin's survey is still useful, though J. D. Bateson's thorough studies a quarter century later remain the standard works.[5] Research on linguistic relations between Rome and Ireland includes studies by Kenneth Jackson, Jane Stevenson, and Damian McManus.[6]

Thanks are due to the many organizations, friends, and colleagues who aided me in the preparation of this book. Both the National Endowment for the Humanities and the American Philosophical Society were instrumental in providing the financial support necessary for research and travel. The libraries and facilities of Harvard University, Washington University, Bowdoin College, Boston University, the American Academy at Rome, and the National Museum of Ireland were invaluable for the work, and I am in debt to their helpful and patient staffs. Special thanks to Susan Rotroff of Washington University and Timothy Bridgman of Trinity College for their many helpful suggestions. But I owe the most gratitude to my wife, Alison Dwyer, who cared for our children Connor and Mackenzie while their father pursued his research in dusty libraries and distant lands.

NOTES

1. I have used standard editions of the well-known classical authors, primarily the widely available Oxford, Teubner, and Loeb series. For the more obscure authors, I have used the best available editions and listed these in the footnotes.

2. Haverfield 1913; MacNeill 1919, 133-60.

3. Kenney 1929, 110-55.

4. Killeen 1976; Tierney 1976; Rivet and Smith 1979.

5. Ó Ríordáin 1947; Bateson 1973, 1976. Other helpful works include Rynne 1976; Warner 1976; Carson and O'Kelly 1977; B. Raftery 1994, 200–219; Freeman 1995.

6. K. Jackson 1953, 76–148; Stevenson 1989; McManus 1983, 1991.

Ireland and the Classical World

CHAPTER ONE

The Archaeology of Roman Material in Ireland

Philology and archaeology ideally should work together to integrate literary and material evidence in the investigation of a particular subject. The investigation of interaction between Ireland and the classical world is no exception, with literary studies aided by physical remains of Roman origin occurring in several dozen Irish sites of the early centuries A.D. The difficulty, as is so often the case, is one of interpretation. Were these objects lost or deposited in antiquity, or is their presence the result of careless medieval collectors or modern antiquarians? Does a Roman fibula in County Dublin necessarily point to manufacture in Roman Britain or the continent, or might an itinerant Gaulish craftsman in Ireland, or even a Roman-inspired Irish jeweler, have made the object?

Surveys of Roman material in Ireland include those of Haverfield and Ó Ríordáin in 1913 and 1947 respectively, but the most complete current study is that of J. D. Bateson from 1973.[1] Using Bateson's reasonable criteria, only a fraction of the many classical objects, especially coins, found in Ireland can be judged as acceptable evidence from antiquity. Much of the rest must be rejected due to uncertainties of origin or inadequate records, while confident judgment on other artifacts cannot presently be made. How these objects came to Ireland, whether by way of Roman merchants or visitors, refugees from Britain, returning Irish raiders, or other means, is also a difficult problem in which speculation is often the only option. Nevertheless, a brief look at some of the more interesting Roman finds and their testimony for general patterns of distribution in the first through early fifth centuries A.D. can be fruitful for understanding the relations between Ireland and the classical world (see Figs. 1 and 2).

PRE-ROMAN MATERIAL

Contact between Ireland and the Mediterranean undoubtedly began before the Roman period, but pre-Roman artifacts are few and often of questionable origin. Such finds include Bronze Age double-axes and faience beads of respective Aegean and Egyptian manufacture.[2] A barbary ape skull dated to the last few centuries B.C. was unearthed 5 kilometers southwest of Armagh at the site of Navan, also known as Emain Macha, famous in early Irish literature as the capital of the Ulaid (Ptolemy's *Woluntioi*). The barbary ape was native to north Africa and thus indicates at least indirect trade routes connecting Ireland and the western Mediterranean in the centuries before Roman advances into the British Isles.[3] Four small bronze figurines in the National Museum in Dublin dating from the second to first centuries B.C. also indicate early trade between Italy and Ireland. The four include an Etruscan warrior found in County Roscommon, a robed Etruscan figure from County Sligo, and two Hercules figures of unspecified provenience.

FIRST-CENTURY MATERIAL

The majority of Roman material of the first century A.D. is found, not surprisingly, along the east coast facing Roman Britain, although some artifacts have been unearthed farther inland and on the northern coast. A tiny sherd of first-century A.D. Arretine ware of Italian origin was found inland from the coast at Ballinderry, County Offaly, while a sherd of south Gaulish Samian ware, a brooch, and a Roman bronze fibula, all from the first century A.D., were found, respectively, in Counties Tyrone, Dublin, and Armagh.[4] Another first-century Samian ware fragment, along with other Roman items, comes from the Drumanagh promontory at Loughshinny, 20 kilometers north of Dublin.[5] Of additional interest are the first- to second-century A.D. burial objects from the small island of Lambay, five kilometers off the coast of County Dublin, where a number of fibulae, a beaded torque, bronze discs, and other objects of arguably British origin were recovered from several inhumation burials.[6] A commercial connection with the *Brigantes* tribe across the Irish Sea in central Britain, and

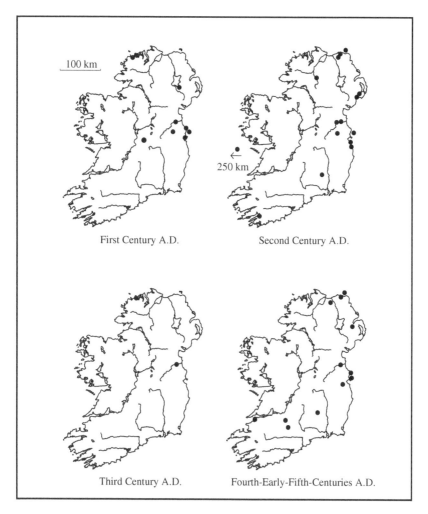

FIGURE I. Roman Archaeological Finds in Ireland (Accepted Finds of Fixed Date)

possibly even identification of the site with Brigantian refugees, are feasible, especially given the crushing defeat of the *Brigantes* by the Romans in A.D. 74.[7]

A key site with Roman material dating from the first through fourth centuries A.D. is the Brug na Bóinne, a sacred mound at Newgrange on the Boyne River. This Neolithic tumulus has yielded coinage from emperors from Domitian (A.D. 81–96) to Arcadius (A.D. 383–408) and numerous

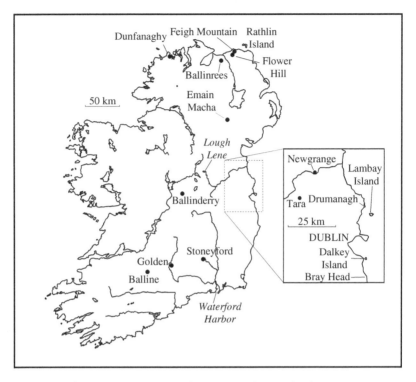

FIGURE 2. Place-name Locations of Roman Finds in Ireland

other precious objects suggesting ritual deposition by pilgrims of Roman times (see Figs. 3, 4, 5, and 6).[8] Whether these depositions were exotic imports left by native Irish, personal offerings by Roman visitors, or both is an open question. These offerings are perhaps not surprising given the impressive presence of the mound, even before modern reconstruction, and its later association in medieval Irish literature with the Dagda (Old Irish "good god"), leader and father figure of the otherworldly Tuatha Dé Danann. One notable artifact is the hook end of a late-second-millennium B.C. Irish gold torque reworked and inscribed by a literate visitor with the Roman letters *SCBONS.MB*, the exact significance of which is unclear, but perhaps indicating the owner's name (see Fig. 6). Excavations seventeen kilometers southwest of Newgrange at Tara, traditional seat of the High Kings of Ireland, have also yielded imported objects from throughout most of the Roman period, such as Samian ware pottery and a lead seal.[9]

SECOND-CENTURY MATERIAL

One of the most intriguing and possibly significant finds of the Roman period does not come technically from Ireland, but from the waters of the Porcupine Bank 250 kilometers west of the island.[10] This find is a Roman *olla*, or storage jar, with an incised Latin graffito, dredged by a Welsh

FIGURE 3. Roman Denarius from the Reign of Domitian (A.D. 81–96) Found at Newgrange
(Photo: Copyright © National Museum of Ireland)

FIGURE 4. Roman Gold Coin from Newgrange from the Reign of Constantine II (A.D. 317–340) Reworked as a Jewelry Pendant
(Photo: Copyright © National Museum of Ireland)

FIGURE 5. Roman Gold Solidus from the Reign of Arcadius (A.D. 383–408)
Found at Newgrange
(Photo: Copyright © National Museum of Ireland)

FIGURE 6. Late-Second-Millennium B.C. Irish Gold
Torque from Newgrange Inscribed with the Roman
Letters SCBONS.MB
(Photo: Copyright © National Museum of Ireland)

trawler. The jar is unlikely to be later than the second century A.D. and was
possibly among the cargo of a storm-tossed merchant ship from Gaul or
Britain. We should not see the jar as necessarily supporting the enigmatic
boast of Juvenal that Rome had advanced its might "beyond the shores of
Ireland" (ultra litora Iuvernae), but this modest find is important in arguing
the veracity of the literary evidence for Hiberno-Roman commerce.[11]

Other second-century finds suggesting the types of wares carried by
Roman merchants to Ireland are a patera, or libation bowl, from Rathlin
Island off the north coast of County Antrim, and Gaulish Samian ware
sherds, one inscribed by the potter DOECCUS, from Dalkey Island at the
southern edge of Dublin Bay.[12] Roman or Roman-influenced burials of
roughly this same period have been discovered on the coast just south of
Dublin Bay at Bray Head, County Wicklow and inland at Stoneyford near
the River Nore in County Kilkenny. The Bray Head skeletons each had a

coin on or near the breast, approximating the Greek and Roman practice of placing a coin in a corpse's mouth to pay the ferryman Charon for the journey across the Styx.[13] The Stoneyford burial, not far from Waterford Harbor, is a classic Roman cremation using a glass urn, suggesting the possible presence of a Roman trading post in southern Ireland in the second century A.D.[14]

Two hoards of several hundred Roman coins each were found early in the nineteenth century on the northern Irish coast at Feigh Mountain and Flower Hill, County Antrim.[15] Both date to the late second century A.D. and consist of denarii silver coins. Such hoards might be expected in later Roman times, when the literature speaks of Irish raids on Britain and possible Irish mercenaries in service to the empire, but the documentary evidence is silent on the mystery of these second-century caches.

THIRD-CENTURY MATERIAL

There is a curious gap in the record of third-century A.D. Roman materials in Ireland, with the discovery of only a few silver and copper coins from Dunfanaghy, County Donegal and Newgrange. This hiatus may be a coincidence that will be revealed by further excavations, or it may be a genuine disruption due to turmoil such as civil wars, the breaching of the Rhine and Danube frontiers by various Germanic tribes, the seizure and rule of parts of the western empire by usurpers, or the beginnings of foreign raids on Britain. This archaeological discontinuity corresponds to an absence of literary references to Ireland in the classical sources of the same century, from Solinus (c. A.D. 200) to the anonymous *Panegyric on Constantius Caesar* (A.D. 297). However, the third century is notable for a paucity of Latin literature in general, so a corresponding absence of literary and archaeological evidence on Ireland during this period need not be significant.

FOURTH- AND EARLY-FIFTH-CENTURY MATERIAL

Two fourth- to early-fifth-century A.D. hoards from Ballinrees, County Londonderry and Balline, County Limerick, better conform to the literary evidence of *Hiberni* and *Scotti* raids on Britain.[16] The Ballinrees hoard consists of more than 1,500 late Roman coins and over 200 ounces of silver ingots and dining ware probably deposited around A.D. 420–25. Two of the ingots have stamped inscriptions, the first reading *CVR MISSI*,

FIGURE 7. Inscribed Silver Ingots from Balline, County Limerick (Late Fourth/
Early Fifth Century A.D.)
(Photo: Copyright © National Museum of Ireland)

perhaps for *CURATOR MISSIONUM* ("quartermaster"), the second, *EX
OFF(ICINA) PATRICI* ("from the workshop of Patricius"). The Balline
cache of the late fourth or early fifth century A.D., found in a gravel pit
in 1940, contains a number of silver ingots and dishes, but no coins (see
Fig. 7). Three of the four Balline ingots are stamped with inscriptions: *EX
O(FFICINA) NON; EX OFFI(CINA) ISATIS;* and *EX XP OF(FI)C(INA)
VILIS,* the last notably bearing the Christian Chi-Rho symbol. Similar
stamps found in Kent suggest a possible southeast British origin for the
Ballinrees and Balline hoards.

Two intriguing finds that cannot be firmly dated to a particular century of the Roman period are an inscribed oculist's stamp from Golden,

County Tipperary, and a boat of possible Mediterranean type from Lough Lene, County Westmeath. Oculist or collyrium stamps are imprint seals used by eye doctors during Roman times to personalize sticks of medicinal salves of vegetable or mineral origin made to combat eye diseases. They are frequently found in Gaul, Germany, and Britain. The Golden stamp, unique to Ireland, was recovered in 1842 from a dike that also contained human bones.[17] The oculist's inscription,

MIVVENTVTIANI(?)C
DIAMYSVSADVCIC

may be read as

MARCI JUVENTI TUTIANI COLLYRIUM
DIAMYSUS AD VETERES CICATRICES

Of Marcus Juventus Tutianus a copperas
eye salve for old scars

This stamp of fine-grained slate may be booty from a raid or a random trade object, but it may also indicate, along with the Stoneyford burial mentioned above, a Roman presence in the river valleys of southern Ireland. Roman contact with Lough Lene, inland from the east coast but connected to it by the Boyne River system, is suggested by the remains of a small wooden boat from antiquity using Mediterranean construction techniques.[18] This craft is similar to several provincial Roman boats unearthed in the Netherlands, Britain, and Germany dating from the first through third centuries A.D., and it implies either an Irish craftsman trained in Mediterranean techniques or Roman manufacture. This small vessel was perhaps commissioned by merchants of the eastern Irish coast for use on inland waterways.

In general, the archaeological evidence of Roman contact with Ireland agrees with the literary testimony of Roman trade with Ireland as well as Irish raids on Britain. Most artifacts of Roman origin occur on islands, in coastal areas, or in river valleys of the east coast facing Britain, locations naturally favored by merchants for ease of access and relative security. As Tacitus says, it was the approaches and harbors that were known by merchants sailing to Ireland for commerce.[19] The hoards of Roman coins in Ireland from the fourth and fifth centuries A.D. also correspond to the literary evidence of Irish raids on late Roman Britain, but less-intrusive explanations of these hoards, such as cached payment for mercenary services or the hasty departure of a local Roman merchant, are equally possible. The archaeological evidence cannot currently prove whether there were ever Roman traders residing in Ireland on a permanent basis, but such a presence cannot be ruled out.

NOTES

1. Bateson adds several more items that he judges as genuine in a subsequent article (1976). The entire volume of *Proceedings of the Royal Irish Academy* 76C, nos. 6–15, is a collection of important papers from the 1974 Colloquium on Hiberno-Roman Relations and Material Remains. Many of the scattered studies on Roman remains in Ireland may be found in the bibliographical listings of both Bateson articles. Only a selection of finds listed by Bateson (1973; 1976) as acceptable are included in this discussion. Similar problems of origin and interpretation arise when considering the few finds of Roman coins in even more distant Iceland (Shetelig 1949).

2. Piggott 1953; Stone and Thomas 1956.

3. Lynn 1986, 16; Mallory and McNeill 1991, 119–20, 146; B. Raftery 1994, 79.

4. Bateson 1973, 29, 63, 66–67; Bateson 1976, 173–74. Arretine ware from Tuscany was considered elegant and refined compared to the more common Samian ware of largely Gaulish manufacture.

5. Bateson 1973, 70; B. Raftery 1994, 206–8; B. Raftery 1996. The London *Sunday Times* (21 January 1996) created a misleading media frenzy when it announced that the discovery of secret Roman artifacts from Drumanagh proved Ireland was "invaded by Romans" and extended "the known limits of the Roman Empire." As Professor Michael Herity responded days later (24 January 1996) in the *Irish Times*, there is no evidence to indicate a Roman invasion or even a bridgehead at Drumanagh, in spite of the fact that many of these first/second century A.D. Drumanagh artifacts (copper ingots, jewelry, coins, etc.) are not as yet public (for legal reasons). As Raftery (1996) notes, the significance of the Roman finds at Drumanagh is difficult to determine without a closer examination of the artifacts than is currently possible, though the known evidence does not suggest a Roman military presence at the site. Media hyperbole should not misrepresent the significance of what is surely an important, but not revolutionary, addition to the material evidence for Roman contact with Ireland.

6. Ó Ríordáin 1947, 54–56; Bateson 1973, 68–70; Lloyd-Morgan 1976, 217–22; Rynne 1976, 231–44; B. Raftery 1994, 200–203.

7. Tacitus *Agricola* 17.

8. Bateson 1973, 46–47, 70–71; Carson and O'Kelly 1977; B. Raftery 1994, 210–11. Less-elaborate artifacts have also been excavated at the nearby monumental site of Knowth (Bateson 1973, 67–68).

9. Bateson 1973, 71–72; B. Raftery 1994, 212.

10. Ó Ríordáin 1947, 65–66; Bateson 1973, 77.

11. Juvenal (*Satire* 2.159–61), Tacitus (*Agricola* 24), and Ptolemy (*Geography* 1.11) refer to merchants visiting Ireland during the early centuries A.D.

12. Bateson 1973, 66–67.

13. Ibid., 45; Warner 1976, 275; B. Raftery 1994, 209. The coins are described as belonging to the reigns of Trajan (A.D. 98–117) and Hadrian (A.D. 117–38).

14. Bateson 1973, 72–73; Warner 1976, 274, 277–78; Bourke 1989; B. Raftery 1994, 206–7.

15. Bateson 1973, 44–45.

16. Mattingly and Pearce 1937; Ó Ríordáin 1947, 43–53, 77–78; Bateson 1973, 42–43, 63–64, 73–74; Bateson 1976, 171–73; B. Raftery 1994, 214–17. For fourth- and fifth-century A.D. raids on Roman Britain, see the *Nomina provinciarum omnium* 13; Pacatus *Panegyric on Theodosius* 5.2; Ammianus Marcellinus *History* 20.1.1, 26.4.5, 27.8.5; Claudian *Panegyric on the Third Consulship of the Emperor Honorius* 54–56, *Panegyric on the Fourth Consulship of the Emperor Honorius* 8.30–33, *On Stilicho's Consulship* 2.247–55, *Gothic War* 416–18, *Epithalamium of Palladius* 88–90. Ammianus Marcellinus (*History* 27.8) specifically mentions the recovery of booty stolen by Attacotti and Scotti raiders in southern Britain.

17. Bateson 1973, 74; R. Jackson 1990; B. Raftery 1994, 218–19. Horace (*Satire* 1.5.30) and other ancient writers mention collyrium as an eye medication.

18. Brindley and Lanting 1990, 10–11; B. Raftery 1994, 208–9.

19. Tacitus *Agricola* 24.

CHAPTER TWO

Language

THE INFLUENCE OF LATIN
IN PRE-PATRICIAN IRELAND

Roman coins, foreign pottery sherds, and exotic burial goods all yield important archaeological evidence for contact between the Mediterranean and pre-Christian Ireland, but evidence of Latin connections to early Irish vocabulary and literacy can also illuminate relations between Rome and Ireland. This linguistic influence consists of a handful of likely commercial terms borrowed into early Irish from Roman traders, as well as the possible inspiration for the native Irish writing system, Ogam, in the Latin grammarians of the late empire. Unfortunately, there is no absolute proof that either Latin loan-words or the influence of the Roman grammatical tradition reached Ireland before the time of St. Patrick; still, a reasonable argument may be made for the presence of both.

LATIN LOAN-WORDS IN EARLY IRISH

Whenever there are trading contacts between cultures, ancient or modern, that speak different languages, language interchange and bilingualism occur to a certain degree. Archaeological evidence, as discussed in the previous chapter, confirms at least a minimal level of such commerce between the Roman empire and Ireland from the first through the early fifth centuries A.D. and argues for the presence of at least one literate Roman in Ireland, given the inscribed Irish torque at Newgrange.[1] In addition, the literary testimony of Tacitus and Ptolemy concerning merchant traffic supports the material evidence of a Roman presence in Ireland during these years.[2] A limited bilingualism, at least by a few merchants from either side of the Irish Sea, would have been essential for commercial transactions and sufficient for the transmission of Latin terms into the vocabulary of early Irish. A model for such interaction in another Celtic land on a much larger scale may be seen at the trading center of Massalia near the mouth of the Rhône River in southern Gaul, where for centuries traders from Gaul, Italy, Greece, and elsewhere in the Mediterranean brought their goods for exchange. Varro says the inhabitants of this city became *trilingues* ("trilingual"), speaking Greek, Latin, and Gaulish.[3] The language of commercial interaction between the Roman world and Ireland need not have been restricted to Latin and Irish in all cases. The Celtic-speaking British and their linguistic cousins from Gaul may have traded directly with Ireland using their own languages and/or Irish. However, given that the primary language of commerce in nearby Roman Britain was apparently Latin, the foreign tongue most used by traders visiting Ireland would probably have been Latin as well.

Other avenues of Latin vocabulary transference to early Irish are also possible. St. Patrick in his autobiographical *Confession* relates that Irish raiders brought back thousands of slaves from Britain in the late fourth and early fifth centuries A.D., many of whom undoubtedly spoke at least some Latin.[4] The influence of Christian Latin may also have been present in Ireland even before Patrick's arrival, given that Pope Celestine I reportedly sent Palladius "to the *Scotti* [Irish] believing in Christ" (*ad Scottos in Christum credentes*) in 431.[5] Contact between Irish settlers in Roman Wales in the late classical period and their kindred in Ireland is another possible channel for the transmission of Latin terms to early Irish.[6]

The methods for dating possible Latin loan-words into early Irish rely on linguistic chronology, semantics, and educated conjecture. The Irish language underwent a notorious series of rapid and radical linguistic changes in the first few centuries A.D., including sound shifts and syllable loss. Loan-words from Latin borrowed into Irish before a particular change took place shared in this transformation, whereas those borrowed at a later period did not. Dating these various linguistic changes can give the latest possible date for the borrowing of a particular loan-word. As an example from the classical languages, Latin *oliva* ("olive") was borrowed from Greek *ἐλαίϝα* (*elaiwa*), later ἐλαία (*elaia*), at a time when the *w* sound, represented by the digamma (ϝ), was still present in the loaning Greek dia-

Table 1. *Old Irish Words Borrowed from Latin*

Latin word	Old Irish word	Meaning
panna	cann	can, vessel
purpura	corcur	purple dye
denarius	dírna	large mass, weight
vinum	fín	wine
aurum	ór	gold

lect.[7] Thus Latin *oliva* ($<$ **olaiva* $<$ **elaiva* $<$ **ἐλαίϝα*) contains a *v*, pronounced *w*. Since intervocalic *w* had disappeared by at least the fourth century B.C. in all Greek dialects, Latin must have borrowed the word prior to this date.[8] Likewise, Irish must have borrowed Latin *planta* ("seedling, offspring") at an early period when the language had no *p*, as it substituted the nearest native equivalent k^w (a linguistic symbol for the sound *q*), yielding *$^*k^w$landa* and thus, with the shift of k^w to *k* and the loss of final syllables, Old Irish *cland* (the *k* sound was represented by *c* in Old Irish, as it is in Latin). By the middle of the sixth century A.D., the Irish had learned to comfortably pronounce *p* and thus adopted the sound directly in later Latin loan-words, such as Old Irish *Pádraig* from Latin *Patricius*.[9]

The exact dating of linguistic changes is difficult, but some developments of early Irish in the fifth and sixth centuries A.D. include apocope (the loss of final syllables—c. 500), the merger of labio-velar k^w into velar *k* (c. 500–550), the acceptance of *p* into Irish speech (c. 500–550), and syncope (the loss of certain internal syllables—c. 550).[10] Unfortunately, all of these diagnostic changes postdate the collapse of Roman power and the advent of St. Patrick, and therefore lie beyond the period covered in this study. To identify potential Latin loan-words of the earlier Roman period, then, deduction based on additional evidence such as trade is necessary. Some possible Latin loan-words into pre-Patrician Irish are shown in Table 1.[11]

Although the words shown in Table 1 are early borrowings from Latin, which had previously borrowed several words from Greek and from other Mediterranean merchants, Irish did not necessarily adopt any of them in the pre-Patrician period. They are simply likely candidates for transference during the Roman period given semantic, comparative, and archaeological evidence.

Irish *cann* ("can, vessel") displays the early substitution of k^w ($> c$) for *p*, as a probable loan from late Latin *panna*, especially given similar borrowings by Gaulish (*panna*) and Welsh (*pann*).[12] The number of Samian ware pottery sherds found in Ireland certainly confirms that Roman vessels were imported by the Irish from the first century A.D.[13] Irish *corcur* ("purple dye") derives from Latin *purpura*, itself a loan from Semitic by way of Greek πορφύρα (*porphyra*).[14] The Romans may have exported finished purple cloth to Ireland as well as stimulated the development of a native dye-producing industry. The discovery of a seventh-century A.D. workshop on Inishkea North, County Mayo, that extracted dye from the shells of the *purpura lapillus* confirms the existence of an early, perhaps Roman-inspired, industry for the production of purple dye in Ireland.[15] The early transfer of Latin *denarius* into Irish as *dírna* ("large mass, weight used as a standard") is probable given Roman *denarii* coins found in Ireland dating from the first few centuries A.D., especially on the northern and eastern coasts.[16] Irish *fín* ("wine") was certainly borrowed at an early date from Latin *vinum*, itself an early borrowing from a common Mediterranean term that also yielded Greek οἶνος (*oinos*) and Hebrew *yayin*. Wine was an extremely popular trade item among the continental Celts from the time of first contact with the classical world, and an extension of the wine trade to Ireland from even pre-Roman times is quite possible.[17] Finally, Latin *aurum* (Old Latin **ausom*) is the source for Old Irish *ór* ("gold"), although gold was mined in ancient Ireland and used masterfully in native crafts long before Roman trade began.

THE OGAM ALPHABET AND THE LATIN GRAMMATICAL TRADITION

Another avenue of Latin influence in pre-Patrician Ireland is the possible origin of the Irish Ogam writing system in the Roman grammatical tradition. A heated controversy over the foreign inspiration for Ogam has existed for over a century, with favorite contenders including the Roman, Greek, Etruscan, and Runic alphabets. The problem has not been solved with certainty, but current scholarly opinion has largely settled on Ogam's invention by an innovative Irishman familiar with the Latin grammarians of the later empire. There is nothing inherently unlikely in the proposal that a wandering Irish student of the fourth century A.D. or earlier may have studied Latin grammar in the schools of Roman Britain or Gaul, then returned to his native land to create an alphabet for the Irish language. Such a character certainly would not have been the first Celt to take up writing. From at least the third century B.C., Celtic speakers from Italy, Gaul, Iberia, and Asia Minor were using various forms of the Roman, Greek, Iberian, and Etruscan alphabets to write in their native tongues or in foreign languages, or both, as in the second-century B.C. Gaulish-Latin bilingual inscription from Todi in Umbria.[18] The Gaulish-language corpus from both northern Italy and Transalpine Gaul includes dedicatory inscriptions, magical charms, memorial stones, an elaborate calendar, and amorous graffiti written in various Greek, Roman, and Etruscan-derived scripts from the second century B.C. to fourth century A.D.[19] Lepontic-speaking Celts of Cisalpine Gaul also left behind a few inscriptions in a variety of the North Etruscan alphabet, most commonly funerary inscriptions.[20] Celt-Iberians, primarily in the second and first centuries B.C., used both the semisyllabic Iberian script and Roman characters to write legal, funerary, and religious inscriptions.[21] Unfortunately, no proven Celtic-language writings survive from the Galatians of Asia Minor or the British.[22]

The Greek and Roman authors provide several important passages relating to writing and classical education among the Celts. In the first century B.C., Caesar speaks of finding a census of the Gaulish Helvetii written out in Greek letters, as were public and private records by other Gaulish tribes, excepting the sacred oral teachings of the druids.[23] Diodorus Siculus relates that the Gauls would cast letters to their deceased relatives on funeral pyres, thinking that the dead would be able to read them.[24] Roman education also spread quickly among the native Celts. By the time of Tiberius in the early first century A.D., the young nobles of the Gallic provinces were studying Latin grammar.[25] Tacitus records that in the late first century A.D., Agricola began training the sons of British nobles to supplement the educated Gauls in his government, with the result that a nation that had previously rejected the language of the Romans began to value a classical education.[26] For several centuries thereafter, the study of Latin as well as Greek grammar was part of the standard education for children of the aspiring upper classes in the western Roman provinces. The distinguished fourth-century poet Ausonius, whose Gaulish-speaking father struggled to converse in Latin but not Greek, received his training in Latin and Greek grammar and rhetoric in his native Gaul and taught there at Bordeaux for thirty years.[27] And although he apologizes for his lack of polished style, St. Patrick wrote his *Confession* in the Latin of his youthful British education.[28]

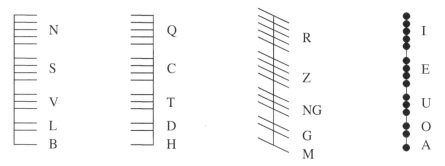

FIGURE 8. The Ogam Alphabet

Thus a young Irishman of means and motivation in the later empire would not have lacked the opportunity to study at least the fundamentals of Latin and even Greek grammar across the sea in Britain or Gaul. But precisely how this hypothetical student from Ireland or one of the Irish colonies in Wales may have used his Roman training to create the Ogam system and record his native tongue remains a mystery. The best current study of the origin of Ogam is found in *A Guide to Ogam* by Damian McManus (1991), to which the discussion below is largely indebted.

Ogam at first glance certainly bears little resemblance to Latin either in form or in arrangement of characters. It is an alphabetic system of twenty horizontal and diagonal strokes and notches written to the right or left of a stem line, with a division into four groups of five letters each.[29] Three of these groups (known in Irish as *aicmi*, plural of *aicme*) are composed of consonants, whereas the fourth contains five vowels. Each letter was assigned a name, the first component of which represented the group of five to which it belonged (*Aicme Beithe, Aicme hÚatha, Aicme Muine, Aicme Ailme*). As the assignment of the names was quite early, they may provide a helpful key in determining the original value of the Ogam consonants. The letters shown in Figure 8 represent the alphabet after the Irish sound shifts of the fifth and sixth centuries, but several of the original sounds were certainly different.[30] The arrangement of Ogam letters will be discussed shortly, but it should be noted that whereas Greek, Latin, Etruscan, and Germanic runes mix vowels and consonants in their alphabetical arrangements, Ogam separates the vowels into a separate group, as do the systems of the classical and Indic grammarians.

Most Ogam inscriptions occur in southern Ireland, though others are found throughout much of the rest of Ireland, on the Isle of Man, and in southwestern Britain (Fig. 9). A number of later Pictish Ogams from the

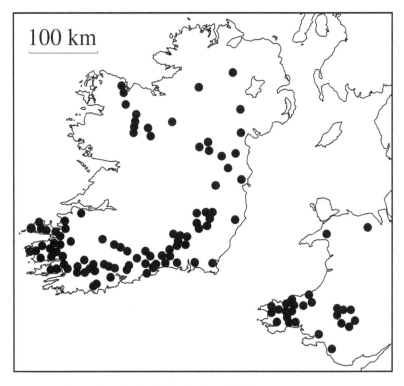

FIGURE 9. Ogam Inscriptions in Ireland and Wales

seventh to ninth centuries also occur in Scotland. The majority of surviving Ogam inscriptions of Ireland and Britain date from the fifth (or possibly late fourth) to early seventh centuries A.D., though knowledge of the alphabet and its use in the manuscript tradition continued for many centuries thereafter.[31] The cumbersome orthography of Ogam would make it a poor literary tool, but it is well designed for short inscriptions carved on stone or wood, with the edge of the medium serving as the stem line. Thus it is no surprise that most surviving Ogams are short and simple stone monuments commemorating honored dead, much like modern tombstones. A common formula is *(the stone) of X son of Y*, with all words in the genitive case, as in *GRILAGNI MAQI SCILAGNI*, "(the stone) of Grilagnas son of Scilagnas."[32]

The origin of the Ogam alphabet, though generally conceded to lie in the Latin grammatical tradition, is in many ways a scholarly puzzle with numerous unsolved and perhaps unsolvable elements. The form of the signary itself, with its various notches and lines, is certainly not related to any other alphabet, whether classical or Germanic. It is a simple system of consecutively increasing marks in groups of five, resembling nothing so much as a row of numerals used for computation, as are Egyptian (| = 1, || = 2, ||||| = 5, etc.), Roman (I = 1, II = 2, V = 5, etc.), and many other numerical systems. Thus it seems a reasonable deduction that the inventor of Ogam appropriated the form of a common counting system for the script of his alphabet.[33]

Although the origin of Ogam's form may be fairly clear, the inspiration for the arrangement of sounds in the signary is obscure and controversial, even among the majority of scholars who accept a genesis in the Roman grammatical tradition. The medieval Irish had their own theories about the origin of Ogam, including the story of Fénius Farrsaid, a learned sage who established a headquarters at the Tower of Babel and collected the best forms of the dispersed languages to create Irish and the Ogam alphabet.[34] More recent scholarly proposals have located the inspiration of the arrangement in Greek, Germanic, or Latin traditions, with runic and Roman sources attracting the most supporters. There are several reasons for proposing that Ogam derived from Germanic runes, including common elements of magical associations, deviation from the classical alphabet sequence, and almost exclusive epigraphical function.[35] However, the written word has magical properties in many cultures, as shown by the ubiquitous charm and curse tablets of the ancient world. In addition, while Ogam and runes both deviate in the sequences of their letters from the order of classical alphabets, their own sequences are not at all similar.[36] Finally, epigraphical writing was common in all periods among the Greeks, Etruscans, and Romans and was certainly not restricted to northern Europe.

If the Ogam *aicmi* derived from the Roman grammatical tradition of the later empire, as most scholars believe, which grammarian was the source? The *Ars maior* of the mid-fourth-century grammarian Donatus, teacher of St. Jerome and master of grammar to Dante, is frequently mentioned in this context.[37] However, grammar was widely studied and codified by the Greeks and Romans many centuries before Donatus. In the fourth century B.C., Plato divides the sounds of Greek into three classes:[38]

> ἀρ' οὖν καὶ ἡμᾶς οὕτω δεῖ πρῶτον μὲν τὰ φωνήεντα διελέσθαι, ἔπειτα τῶν
> ἑτέρων κατὰ εἴδη τά τε ἄφωνα καὶ ἄφθογγα, οὑτωσὶ γάρ που λέγουσιν οἱ
> δεινοὶ περὶ τούτων, καὶ τὰ αὖ φωνήεντα μὲν οὔ, οὐ μέντοι γε ἄφθογγα.
> (*Cratylus* 424C)

Table 2. *The Sound System of Dionysius Thrax*

Vowels (φφωνήεντα)	α	ε	η	ι	ο	υ	ω	
Diphthongs (δίφθογγοι)	αι	αυ	ει	ευ	οι	ου		
Semivowels (ἡμίφωνα)	ζ	ξ	ψ	λ	μ	ν	ρ	σ
Mutes (ἄφωνα)	β	γ	δ	κ	π	τ	θ	φ	χ

Must we not also then first separate out the vowels, then by type the consonants or mutes, as they are called by those who study them, as well as those sounds which are neither vowels nor mutes?

Aristotle a few years later also divides human speech into these three parts: vowels (φφωνήεντα), semivowels (ἡμίφωνα), and mutes (ἄφωνα).[39] In the late second century B.C., the Alexandrian teacher Dionysius Thrax condensed the work of previous linguistic scholars into his *Technē grammatikē*, which became the standard textbook of Greek grammar and greatly influenced Latin grammarians. Dionysius adds a diphthong series to the classes of sounds, but otherwise maintains the divisions of Plato and Aristotle (see Table 2).[40]

Roman grammarians continued Dionysius' Greek system with only a few changes, such as dropping the diphthong series, adding a class of *Graecae litterae*, or Greek letters, for those sounds not part of the standard Latin alphabet, such as *y* and *z* (Greek υ and ζ), and including Latin *q* among the mutes. Varro in the first century B.C. writes of the division of consonants (*consonantes*) between semivowels (*semivocales*) and mutes (*mutae*) in a fragment of his *De lingua Latina*.[41] In the next century, Remmius Palaemon wrote the first comprehensive Latin grammatical treatise, while Quintilian warned against neglecting the basics of grammar, such as learning the difference between vowels (*vocales*), semivowels (*semivocales*), and mutes (*mutae*).[42] Roman grammarians of imperial times taught in every city of the Latin-speaking world, many producing their own versions of an *Ars grammatica* as textbooks for students. Among those grammarians surviving from the third and fourth centuries who deal with the basics of phonology are Charisius, Diomedes, and Dositheus, but none attained the influence and readership of Aelius Donatus.[43] His elementary *Ars minor* and more advanced *Ars maior* had rapidly become the standard texts of Latin grammar by the late fourth century, and by the early fifth century were inspiring commentaries of their own, including a study by Servius.[44]

Table 3. *The Sound System of Donatus*

Vowels (*vocales*)	*a*	*e*	*i*	*o*	*u*				
Semivowels (*semivocales*)	*f*	*l*	*m*	*n*	*r*	*s*	*x*		
Mutes (*mutae*)	*b*	*c*	*d*	*g*	*h*	*k*	*p*	*q*	*t*
Greek letters (*Graecae litterae*)	*y*	*z*							

Donatus' *Ars minor* omits material on letters and sounds, but the phonology chapter of his *Ars maior* continues the earlier division into vowels, semivowels, mutes, and Greek letters, and may be taken as the standard system for most Roman grammarians (see Table 3).[45]

But how could the Roman division of sounds into vowels, semivowels, mutes, and Greek letters be reworked to produce the Ogam system, which seems at first glance to have no linguistic logic to its divisions aside from a separate vowel series? There is no consensus on the method used by Ogam's inventor other than the obvious separation of vowels and some phonetic pairings. However, if one sees the classical grammatical tradition as the inspiration and starting-point for Ogam rather than as its genetic ancestor, the difficulties are minimized.[46] Table 4 (step one) shows the result of using the sound system of Donatus and removing the consonants *k*, *p*, and *x* and the vowel *y*, sounds that were redundant or absent in fourth-century Irish. This leaves the last line rather bare and the others unbalanced, not a satisfactory outcome if the hypothetical Irish inventor needs five letters in each series to fit his numerical signary. So if *m*, *r*, and *g* are shifted to the bottom, and *b* is moved to the start of the second series, giving the standard *a-b* order of the classical alphabets in the initial letters of the first two series, the outcome is as diagrammed in Table 4 (step two). Add a letter, represented by *ng* in later Ogam, to the last line to stand for early Irish *g*^{w}, then group the letters within each series by similar sounds in alphabetic order (*d* and *t*, *c* and *q*, *g* and *ng*), and the result is the Ogam alphabet (see Table 4, step three).[47]

Of course, this is not to say that Ogam's originator necessarily followed the steps outlined above, merely that an Irishman with training in the basics of classical grammar would have had no great difficulty in adapting the Latin grammatical system into the Ogam alphabet by similar means.

In theory, an Irishman familiar with Greek or Roman grammar and interested in devising a native alphabet based on a classical fourfold division of sounds could have invented Ogam anywhere in the Hellenistic or

Table 4. *Latin to Ogam*

Step One							
Vowels	*a*	*e*	*i*	*o*	*u*		
Semivowels	*f*	*l*	*m*	*n*	*r*	*s*	
Mutes	*b*	*c*	*d*	*g*	*h*	*q*	*t*
Greek letters	*z*						
Step Two							
	a	*e*	*i*	*o*	*u*		
	b	*f*	*l*	*n*	*s*		
	c	*d*	*h*	*q*	*t*		
	z	*m*	*r*	*g*			
Step Three							
	a	*o*	*u*	*e*	*i*		
	b	*l*	*f*	*s*	*n*		
	h	*d*	*t*	*c*	*q*		
	m	*g*	*ng*	*z*	*r*		

Roman world at any time during or after the third century B.C. If a curious and resourceful Irishman had visited the Greek colony at Massalia, for example, in the late centuries B.C., he could have learned the Greek system of vowels, semivowels, and mutes and adapted it into Ogam by a method comparable to that outlined above. However, an early Greek inspiration for Ogam, while conceivable, is less likely than a later Roman genesis, especially given the fifth-century A.D. date for the earliest Ogam inscriptions.[48] It is also conceivable that Ogam was invented in Ireland under the inspiration of a literate Roman. The previously discussed torque with Latin letters from Newgrange, possible Roman merchant settlements, and hints that Christian communities were present in Ireland before St. Patrick all provide arguments for Latin literacy in early Ireland. But as there is so little evidence for long-term Roman communities in Ireland, and no evidence at all for *Ars grammatica* instruction before the mid-fifth century, such an origin for Ogam again should be classed as possible, but unlikely. Therefore, the third and most feasible method of classical inspiration for Ogam lies in the generally accepted theory of an Irish student training with a Roman grammarian in Britain or Gaul. Irish warriors from the time of Agricola's petty king in the first century A.D. to the fifth-century *Scotti* and *Hiberni* raiders were venturing abroad, and there is no reason why more peaceful Irishmen could not have traveled to Britain and Gaul as well.[49] With several centuries of trade between Rome and Ireland as well as Irish settlements in Wales at the end of the empire, some of the Irish upper classes must have seen the political and economic advantages of at least a rudimentary Latin education for their children. Moreover, if the profound Irish interest in poetry and its grammatical foundations during the Middle Ages is any indication of earlier inclinations, there may have been an eagerness for linguistic education among the Irish of late classical times.[50] Since the earliest surviving Ogam monuments can be dated only to the mid-fifth century in both Ireland and Wales, the invention of Ogam does not necessarily fall within the pre-Patrician boundaries of this study. However, given the amount of time it would have taken for a script to have gained acceptance and spread across Ireland and Wales, the genesis of Ogam in the late Roman period is a strong possibility.

NOTES

1. Bateson 1973, 70–71; Carson and O'Kelly 1977, 51; B. Raftery 1994, 210–11.

2. Tacitus *Agricola* 24; Ptolemy *Geography* 1.11.

3. Isidorus *Etymologiae* 15.1.63.

4. Patrick *Confession* 1.

5. Prosper Tiro *Chronicle* 1307. The date of Patrick's arrival in Ireland and the identity of those who may have preceded him are controversial. See De Paor 1993, 3–50, 70–113.

6. See Dillon 1977; Ó Cathasaigh 1984. Even bilingualism for very limited political relations must have been present at least as early as the first century A.D., when an expatriate Irish king joined the retinue of Agricola (Tacitus *Agricola* 24).

7. An asterisk (*) is used to indicate a reconstructed sound or word not actually attested in any written records.

8. See Buck 1955, 46–52; Sihler 1995, 182–87.

9. K. Jackson 1953, 127; Thurneysen 1980, 570–71.

10. K. Jackson 1953, 142–43; McManus 1983; Koch 1995.

11. This list and commentary are largely based on McManus 1983, 42–45. Other possible early Latin loan-words to Old Irish listed by McManus include: *ancora* > *ingor* ("anchor"); *cista* > *ces* ("basket"); *creterra* > *creithir* ("container, vessel"); *crocus* > *cróch* ("saffron"); *exhibernum* > *esarn* ("year-old wine"); *moneta* > *monad* ("money"); *modius* > *muide* ("vessel"); *piper* > *scibar* ("pepper"); *sextarius* *situla* > *sesra* ("a measure of capacity"); *situla* > *síthal* ("vessel"). See also J. Stevenson 1989, 131–33.

12. Thurneysen 1980, 570; Billy 1993, 118.

13. J. Bateson 1973, 63–77; 1976.

14. K. Jackson 1953, 126; Thurneysen 1980, 570–71; Vendryes 1987, 208–9. According to Servius (*Commentary on Vergil's Aeneid* 8.660), the native Gaulish word for the color purple was *virga*.

15. Henry 1953. Bede (*Historia ecclesiastica* 1) mentions extensive purple-dye production in early medieval Britain.

16. Bateson 1973, 42–48.

17. Diodorus Siculus 5.26; Caesar *Gallic War* 2.15; Thurneysen 1980, 572; K. Jackson 1953, 123; Cunliffe 1988, 71–75, 87–88. Roman pottery found at the Rath of the Synods on the royal hill of Tara, County Meath, may be remains of a goblet and flagons from the first and second centuries A.D. (Bateson 1973, 71–72; B. Raftery 1994, 212).

18. Lambert 1994, 74–76.

19. Lejeune 1985a; 1985b; 1988; Duval and Pinault 1988; Meid 1992; Eska and Evans 1993, 35–43; Lambert 1994.

20. Lejeune 1971; Eska and Evans 1993, 43–46.

21. Lejeune 1955; Eska 1989; Eska and Evans 1993, 30–35.

22. Weisgerber 1931; Eska and Evans 1993, 46–47. Noteworthy, however, are a second-century B.C. graffito written in Greek by four Galatian mercenaries on a temple in Upper Egypt (Dittenberger 1915–24, 757), and two possible British-language curse-tablets from Bath (Tomlin 1987).

23. Caesar *Gallic War* 1.29, 6.14.

24. Diodorus Siculus 5.28.6.

25. Tacitus *Annals* 3.43.

26. Tacitus *Agricola* 21.

27. Ausonius *Epicedion in patrem* 9. For a list of teachers of Latin and Greek at Bordeaux from the third to fifth centuries, see Kaster 1988, 455–62, 467–68.

28. Patrick *Confession* 9.

29. A fifth group, known as the *forfeda* ("supplementary characters"), is a later development. A key source on later Irish views of Ogam is the medieval Irish handbook for poets known as the *Auraicept na nÉces* (Ahlqvist 1982).

30. Hamp 1953, 311–12; McManus 1991, 1–3, 34–41. Ogam *v* was pronounced *w* in the earliest period, but *f* by the seventh century. The original values of *h*, *ng*, and *z* are uncertain, though *y* (as in *yard*), *gw* (as in *guacamole*), and *st*, respectively, are possibilities.

31. McManus 1991, 44–64, 78–100. A bone die from Ballinderry Crannog no. 2 in County Offaly has the number 5 represented by three parallel marks resembling the Ogam letter *V*, identical to the Roman numerical value (Heneken 1942). If this is indeed an Ogam mark intended as a Roman numeral, and if the site can be redated to the second century A.D. (neither of which is certain), the Ballinderry die would represent the oldest surviving Ogam inscription (see J. Raftery 1959, 7; Mac White 1961, 301–2; Carney 1975, 56; McManus 1991, 93–94, 129–30).

32. McManus 1991, 51–52. Aside from inscriptional remains, references to and use of Ogam also occur in Old Irish literature, law, and linguistic texts (ibid., 147–66).

33. Thurneysen 1937; Vendryes 1948; K. Jackson 1953, 156–57; McManus 1991, 6–18. Elaborate appeals for Ogam signary origins to be found in secret druidic hand signals, Roman military codes (see Polybius 10.45–47), or Germanic *hahalruna*, a similarly artificial system of progressively increasing notches (Elliott 1959, 83–86), are unwarranted.

34. *Auraicept na nÉces* 1.1–14 (Ahlqvist 1982, 47–48); McManus 1991, 147–53.

35. For discussion of other arguments for runic origin, see McManus 1991, 23–26.

36. Ogam: *b l v/f s n h d t c q m g ng z r a o u e i*; runes: *f u th a r k g w h n i j ï p z s t b e m l ng o d*.

37. Dante *Paradiso* 12.137–38.

38. See also Plato *Theaetetus* 203B.

39. Aristotle *Poetics* 20.1–4. Aristotle gives *s* and *r* as examples of semivowels, *g* and *d* as examples of mutes.

40. Dionysius Thrax *Technē grammatikē* 6.

41. Pseudo-Sergius *Explanationes in Donatum* 1 (H. Keil, *Grammatici Latini*, 8 vols. [Leipzig, 1855–1923], 4: 520).

42. Suetonius *De grammaticis* 23; Quintilian *Institutio oratoria* 1.4.6.

43. Charisius *Ars grammatica* 1 (*Grammatici Latini* 1: 7–11); Diomedes *Ars grammatica* 2 (*Grammatici Latini* 1: 420–26); Dositheus *Ars grammatica* 4 (*Grammatici Latini* 7: 381–86).

44. Servius *Commentarius in Donatum* (*Grammatici Latini*, vol. 4).

45. Donatus *Ars maior* 1.2 (*Grammatici Latini* 4: 367–68; Holtz 1981, 603–4).

46. Hamp 1953, 310–12; Kurylowicz 1961; Carney 1975, 60–61; Ahlqvist 1982, 8–9; McManus 1991, 24–34.

47. The front (*e i*) and back (*o u*) vowels of Ogam are paired and in reverse order from Donatus, while the noninitial letters inside each series that are not similar sounds (*l* and *f*, *s* and *n*, *z* and *r*) are placed in antialphabetic order. Both of these arrangements, along with the positioning of *b* at the head of the second series and the grouping of similar sounds in alphabetic order, show the inventor's awareness of grammar and the Latin alphabet.

48. Plutarch (*Moralia* 410) records the visit of the Greek grammarian Demetrius of Tarsus to Britain in the first century A.D., whereas the sixth-century Irishman St. Colum Cille correctly associates grammar with Greek origins (*Lebor na Huidre* 1148–51; Ó Cuív 1983, 1–2).

49. Tacitus *Agricola* 24; Pacatus *Panegyric on Theodosius* 5.2; Ammianus Marcellinus *History* 20.1.1, 26.4.5, 27.8.5; Jerome *Adversus Jovinianum* 2.7; Claudian *Panegyric on the Third Consulship of the Emperor Honorius* 54–56, *Panegyric on the Fourth Consulship of the Emperor Honorius* 8.30–33, *On Stilicho's Consulship* 2.247–55, *Gothic War* 416–18, *Epithalamium to Palladius* 88–90.

50. There is no direct testimony concerning Irish poets during the Roman period, but the Celtic bards of Gaul placed great emphasis on eloquence and study (Diodorus Siculus 5.31; Caesar *Gallic War* 6.14; Lucian *Heracles*). See also the *Auraicept na nÉces* (Ahlqvist 1982) and Ó Cuív 1983.

CHAPTER THREE

Ancient Authors

Rufius Festus Avienus

Sources for the *Ora maritima*

It is ironic that the earliest classical reference to Ireland may be contained in a very late document, the *Ora maritima* of Rufius Festus Avienus, who wrote in the mid-fourth century A.D. Avienus served as a Roman pro-consul and composed rather second-rate poetry based on earlier authors. His rambling *Ora maritima* is a *periplus*, or coastal description, over 700 lines long that primarily describes the coast from Gades (Cadiz) in the southwestern Iberian peninsula to Massalia (Marseilles) in Gaul, but with frequent digressions on other parts of western Europe. Avienus apparently drew on a variety of sources, including Greek and Carthaginian records from around 500 B.C. However, the intermixture and uncertainty of Avienus' sources as well as the permutations they may have undergone before reaching him make the *Ora maritima* an extremely problematic source for early Ireland. If, however, the sources for the *Ora maritima* that describe Ireland were genuinely composed in the late sixth or early fifth century B.C., they predate the next surviving classical references to the island by several centuries.

One section of the poem arguably drawing on the earliest sources is a digression beginning at the Oestrymnides Islands, but the location of the islands is itself debatable:[1]

ast hinc duobus in Sacram (sic insulam
dixere prisci) solibus cursus rati est.
haec inter undas multam caespitem iacet,
eamque late gens Hiernorum colit.
propinqua rursus insula Albionum patet.
Tartessisque in terminos Oestrumnidum
negociandi mos erat. Carthaginis
et iam colonis et vulgus inter Herculis
agitans columnas haec adhibant aequora.
quae Himilco Poenus mensibus vix quattuor,
ut ipse semet rem probasse retulit
enavigantem, posse transmitti adserit.

From here it is a two-day voyage to the Sacred Isle,
for by this name the ancients called the island.
It lies rich in turf among the waves,
thickly populated by the *Hierni.*
Nearby lies the island of the *Albiones.*
The Tartessians were accustomed to trade even
to the edge of the Oestrymnides. The Carthaginian
colonists and people around the Pillars
of Hercules frequented these waters.
Four months scarcely is enough for the voyage,
as Himilco the Carthaginian proved
by sailing there and back himself.

The poem claims it is a two-day sail from the Oestrymnides to the *insula sacra* ("Sacred Isle"). The epithet *insula sacra*, if it refers here to Ireland, probably originated with a false etymology, as the oldest Greek name for Ireland, *Iernē* (Ἰέρνη), is similar to the Greek phrase *hiera nēsos* (ἱερὰ νῆσος), "sacred/holy island." If the term originated in the western Greek colony of Massalia, it may have been an even more similar *iera nēsos* (ἱερὰ νῆσος), without the initial *h-*, as Massalia was founded around 600 B.C. by the Ionic Greek-speaking city of Phocaea on the coast of Asia Minor. The East Ionic dialect of Greek lost the aspirant, or *h-*sound, early in its linguistic history, whereas most other Greek dialects (such as the Attic speech of Athens) retained the sound. But to a Greek sailor of any dialect, *Iernē* must have sounded vaguely similar to *(h)iera nēsos.* The association would have been aided by the Greek tradition of distant sacred or supernatural islands to the west, such as Calypso's Ogygie, Scheria of the Phaeacians, or the Isles of the Blessed.[2]

The ancient Irish themselves probably called their island *Iweriu (from an *Iwerion- root), though there is some debate about the exact form used.[3] The name seems to derive ultimately from an Indo-European form *piwer-, meaning "fat, fertile," so that the ancient Irish name for Ireland might be translated "The Fertile Land"—a suitable description given Pomponius Mela's description of Ireland as being so fertile that the cattle grazing there were in danger of bursting from the rich fodder.[4] This holy island is, intriguingly, rich in turf of the kind still burned in Irish cottages today. It is densely populated by the *Hierni*, a name not used for the Irish by any other ancient author, but certainly a reasonable Roman derivative of the Greek *Ierne*.

The neighbors of the *Hierni* in the *Ora maritima* are the *Albiones*, an archaic name for the inhabitants of Britain. Tartessus, whose citizens frequently sailed to the Oestrymnides, was a town and region around the Guadalquivir River in southern Iberia visited by Samnian and Phocaean Greeks as early as the seventh century B.C. (see Fig. 10).[5] The Oestrymnides may be islands off the Brittany coast near Brest or the Scilly Isles off Cornwall, both groups being near coveted ancient tin deposits and a two-day sail from Ireland with a good wind. British historian C.F.C. Hawkes has argued for a more southerly location near the Isla de Ons, just off the northwestern coast of Spain, also a source for tin;[6] but this would, of course, be more than a two-day sail from Ireland. To complicate the matter, members of a tribe on the northern coast of Atlantic Spain were known as the *Albiones* as well. Carthaginian colonists and other seafaring people near the Pillars of Hercules, aside from the Tartessians, apparently visited "these waters" (*haec aequora*) as well, though it is not completely clear if the waters referred to are those around the Oestrymnides or the Sacred Isle. The four months needed for a voyage from southern Spain, according to Avienus, seems excessive unless he refers to a round trip, including time in the British Isles for trade. Carthaginian explorers, such as Himilco, were certainly capable of sailing to Ireland and back at this date, if they had sufficient hope of profitable trade. Pliny briefly mentions Himilco's voyage north beyond Gibraltar, and ancient sources note contemporary Carthaginian voyages of equal and greater distance south along the African coast.[7] Elsewhere in the *Ora maritima*, Avienus relates that Himilco sailed to a

FIGURE 10. The Lands of the *Ora maritima*

foggy, calm region full of seaweed where no mariner had journeyed before and that he recorded the experiences of his voyage.[8]

However, the question of whether Avienus is paraphrasing early Massaliote and/or Carthaginian sources on Ireland in this passage is difficult to answer. There are three arguments commonly made for assigning a very early date to at least some of Avienus' sources. First, the *Ora maritima* as a whole progresses eastward along the coast from Gades in Iberia and ends with glowing praise for Massalia in Gaul. This terminus suggests that Avienus based his poem on an early Massaliote source. Massalia was founded c. 600 B.C., and in subsequent decades established its own colonies in Spain and traded at least as far as Gades and the Tartessus region on the southwestern Atlantic coast of the Iberian peninsula, beyond the Pillars of Hercules. Carthaginian expansion into Spain may have blocked this Atlantic trade by 500 B.C.; thus any Massaliote periplus with descriptions of the Atlantic littoral should predate the Carthaginian blockade. Second, Himilco probably explored north of the Pillars of Hercules in the early fifth century B.C., when the power of Carthage was at its height. Avienus mentions Himilco's voyage several times in the *Ora maritima* and may well be drawing, at least indirectly, on Carthaginians records of the voyage in his references to the *Hierni*.[9] Third, *Albiones*, a name Avienus probably uses for the inhabitants of Britain, was generally superseded by forms based on *Prettan-* or *Brettan-*, perhaps as early as Pytheas' late-fourth-century B.C. voyage. Pliny, later echoed by Bede, says *Albion* was the original name for Britain.[10] Thus if Avienus uses *Albion*, he may be drawing on truly ancient sources.

There are, however, difficulties with these arguments. First, even if Avienus based his poem on a pre-500 B.C. Massaliote periplus, the section mentioning the *Hierni* is a digression from any Gades-to-Massalia coastal description. Unless the hypothetical Massaliote author also included this digression (which would be very unusual in the matter-of-fact Greek periplus genre), it has no necessary claim to Massaliote antiquity. Second, evidence of Carthaginian voyages in the northern Atlantic is limited and questionable, as our knowledge of Himilco's voyage is unfortunately restricted to the material from the *Ora maritima* and the very brief reference by Pliny. This latter record does not inspire great confidence, since in the same passage Pliny claims that sailors from India were shipwrecked near the Suebi in Germany.[11] Finally, it is possible that the term *Albiones* in the *Ora maritima* is not a genuine reference to the inhabitants of Britain from a fifth-century B.C. or earlier source, but an archaizing and poetic usage by Avienus. *Albion* was, after all, a well-known term for Britain used by authors into the Middle Ages.

Thus we are left with many uncertainties concerning Avienus' sources for this section of the *Ora maritima*. It is certainly possible that the Roman poet is drawing on early sources from around 500 B.C. that record the name of the Irish and the facts that they lived on a densely populated island, burned turf to warm themselves, and were at least occasionally visited by Iberian mariners from the Mediterranean region, perhaps even by Greeks or Carthaginians. It is also possible that Avienus is drawing on much later sources and sprinkling his text with archaic names for poetic effect. In the absence of convincing proof one way or the other, we must be cautious, yet open to the possibility that the *Ora maritima* genuinely contains the earliest historical information on Ireland and the Irish.

THE HELLENISTIC GEOGRAPHERS

Between the hypothetical sources of Avienus' *Ora maritima* in the late sixth and early fifth centuries B.C. and the first certain reference to Ireland by Julius Caesar in the mid-first century B.C., a number of Greek geographers wrote about the lands and islands of northwestern Europe. Ephorus (c. 405–330 B.C.), Pytheas (fl. 310–306 B.C.), Timaeus (c. 356–320 B.C.), Eratosthenes (c. 285–194 B.C.), Polybius (c. 200–118 B.C.), and Posidonius (135–51 B.C.) all may have written of Ireland, but unfortunately no direct reference to the island survives in any of their works. This may not be indicative of their knowledge, however, as all but Polybius survive only in a few scattered fragments quoted by later, sometimes hostile, authors.

The thirty-book *History* of Ephorus was known and used by Polybius, Diodorus Siculus, Strabo, and other ancient writers. He is the earliest Greek historian to deal extensively with events to the west of the Greek world, with individual books covering specific geographical areas such as Sicily, Spain, and Gaul. Although he never refers to Ireland in any of the passages attributed to him, his original work may have noted the island and its people.[12]

The early-fifth-century B.C. Himilco may deserve recognition as the first recorded Mediterranean voyager to the area of the British Isles, but the late-fourth-century B.C. travels of Pytheas northward beyond the Pillars of Hercules were more extensive, though only slightly better documented. Although this explorer from Massalia does not mention Ireland or the Irish in the few fragments attributed to him, it is probable that he at least saw the island, even if he did not actually set foot there.[13] His report of the total coastline of Britain, as well as other descriptive details from throughout the island, may imply an extensive reconnaissance if not a circumnavigation of Britain.[14] If he sailed the length of Britain's western coast, he must have at least noticed the peaks of the Antrim Mountains of northern Ireland as he sailed the narrow channel between Ulster and Scotland. Strabo's use of the plural term *Brettanic Isles* (τῶν Βρεττανίδων) in his disparaging comments on Pytheas may go back to the words of the Massaliote geographer himself.[15] If so, Pytheas' use of the plural may directly suggest a knowledge of Ireland, as later writers commonly use the term to indicate both Britain and Ireland.[16] However, the other Brettanic island(s) may be the Cassiterides or Tin Isles, which were known to the Greek world as early as Herodotus in the fifth century B.C.; the mysterious isle of Thule; or the Hebrides.[17]

Several decades after Pytheas' voyage, Timaeus in Sicily wrote his voluminous *Sicilian History*, which covered the history and geography not only of his native land, but also of many areas of the west, including the lands of the Carthaginians, Ligurians, Celts, and Iberians. Like the other Hellenistic geographers, Timaeus does not specifically refer to Ireland in his surviving fragments, but he is the first to note that tin is exported from an island off the southwest coast of Britain, demonstrating that the Greeks knew of commercial activities in the Irish Sea during this period.[18] In the next generation, the great Alexandrian geographer Eratosthenes first laid out the regions of the known world in reasonably accurate measurements of latitude and longitude. He does not directly mention Ireland in any of his surviving fragments, but it is very likely that he included Ireland in his world geography and was thus an important source for Strabo and others who do discuss the island.

In the second century B.C., the historian Polybius deals in great detail and from firsthand experience with the lands and people of the western Mediterranean, including some of the earliest extensive descriptions of the Celts.[19] But he does not trust the reports of Pytheas on the lands to the north of Gaul and says that the merchants of Massalia and even Atlantic Gaul had no detailed information on Britain in his day.[20] He does, however, use the plural for the Brettanic Isles (τῶν Βρεττανικῶν νήσων), though, as with Pytheas, it is not certain if he means to include Ireland among them.[21]

Posidonius, Stoic philosopher and teacher of Cicero, was well acquainted with the Celts of Gaul and provides us with the most extensive description of Celtic customs and beliefs in antiquity in his early-first-century B.C. writings.[22] Yet again, he notes the plural Brettanic Isles without specifically mentioning Ireland.[23] Thus Posidonius, as well as Eratosthenes and the other geographers of the Hellenistic period, provide tantalizing bits of information on Britain and the islands of northwest Europe, and may indeed have known of Ireland, but unfortunately they never directly mention Ireland or the Irish people in their surviving works.

Diodorus Siculus

Diodorus of Sicily, writing between 60 and 30 B.C., composed a universal history that covers events in Greece and the lands beyond from the mythological age of heroes until 60 B.C. Unfortunately, less than half of his original forty books survive, but his existing work is still among the most extensive of any Greek historian from antiquity. The first six books of his history cover the geography and ethnography of the inhabited world from India to the Atlantic, with his descriptions of western Europe drawing on Timaeus, Polybius, and especially Posidonius, but it is difficult to be certain of his exact sources in many sections. In the middle of his description of the Celts of Gaul, he describes the northern and westernmost Celts of the continent as cannibals, similar to the *Prettanoi* or *Brettanoi* (depending on the manuscript) who live in *Iris* (Ἶρις):

> ἀγριωτάτων δ' ὄντων τῶν ὑπὸ τὰς ἄρκτους κατοικούντων καὶ τῶν τῇ Σκυθίᾳ πλησιοχώρων, φασί τινας ἀνθρώπους ἐσθίειν, ὥσπερ καὶ τῶν Πρεττανῶν τοὺς κατοικοῦντας τὴν ὀνομαζομένην Ἶρις. (Diodorus Siculus 5.32.3)

> The most savage tribes are those in the north and those living near Scythia. Some say they eat human flesh, just like the *Prettanoi* inhabiting the land called *Iris*.

It is very tempting to see *Iris* as a reference to Ireland. First, the name seems at least vaguely similar to other names for the island. Second, the inhabitants of Iris are *Prettanoi* or *Brettanoi*, and Ireland was considered one of the Brettanic Isles in antiquity. Ptolemy even calls Ireland "Little Britain" (Μικρὰ Βρεττανία).[24] At the very least, the fact that Diodorus says the island is inhabited by Britons certainly implies that *Iris* is a place very near Britain. Third, those who dwell on *Iris* are cannibals, a favorite derogation aimed at the Irish after the time of Diodorus.[25]

But there are problems in equating Diodorus' *Iris* with Ireland. Although *Iris* superficially seems similar to other ancient names for Ireland, close analysis reveals that it is not, in fact, a near linguistic relative to those other appellations. It is likely that Diodorus or his sources were following the very human habit of substituting a known word for one that was unfamiliar. To a Greek, especially after going through a number of intermediaries, the name of Ireland may have sounded vaguely like the name of the goddess of the rainbow and messenger of the gods, Iris (Ἶρις).[26] She was a relatively minor figure (though she would have been well known to any Greek), and it is unknown why she might be identified with Ireland, though anyone who has spent much time in Ireland may find the association with rain and rainbows a natural one.[27]

Ireland was certainly considered one of the British Isles by the ancients, but no one, aside from this possible reference in Diodorus, ever calls the inhabitants "Britons." They are always *Hiberni*, *Scotti*, or known by individual tribal names. Still, it seems reasonable, especially at this early point in classical knowledge of the Irish, for Diodorus or his sources to think of all inhabitants of the Brettanic Isles as *Brettanoi*, in the way that all those living south of Egypt were Ethiopians to the earliest Greeks. As for cannibalism, the Greeks and Romans did not reserve such a slander just for the Irish. Homer sings that the Laestrygonians dined on Odysseus' men, whereas Herodotus claims the Callatiae of India and the Issedones of Scythia ritually ate their dead fathers and that the Massagetae engaged in cannibalism as well.[28] Pliny relates that the druids of Gaul and other tribes also ate human flesh.[29] Other classical references to cannibalism suggest it was a standard description attached to many barbarians beyond the civilizing influence of Greco-Roman culture.

It is certainly possible that this passage of Diodorus refers to Ireland, but there were other British islands known at least vaguely to the classical world at this time, and, as noted, other lands with a reputation for cannibalism. Nonetheless, the vague similarity of the name to other names for Ireland and the reputation of Irish cannibalism in later classical sources gives the identification with Ireland some credence. But it remained for Diodorus' contemporary, Caesar, to provide the first unequivocal reference to Ireland in the ancient literary sources.

Julius Caesar

In Caesar's account of his second invasion of Britain in 54 B.C., he pauses to provide a brief description of the island and its people. Included in this narrative is a short geographical summary of Britain's shape, size, and location in respect to nearby islands. Fortunately, one of these islands is *Hibernia*, giving us our first certain and datable reference to Ireland in classical literature:

> *alterum vergit ad Hispaniam atque occidentem solem; qua ex parte est Hibernia, dimidio minor, ut aestimatur, quam Britannia, sed pari spatio transmissus atque ex Gallia est in Britanniam. in hoc medio cursu est insula, quae appellatur Mona.* (*Gallic War* 5.13)

> The second side of Britain faces Hispania and the west, in which direction is *Hibernia*, smaller by one-half, as it is estimated, than Britain. The separation is equal to that of Britain from Gaul. In the middle of the channel is an island called *Mona*.

Caesar's *Hibernia* became the dominant Latin name for Ireland from the first century B.C. to medieval times and beyond. The pronunciation of initial *h* in Latin was waning even in the time of Caesar and was soon thereafter used only by educated and socially conscious Latin speakers (the average Roman would have called Ireland *Ibernia* throughout the classical period).[30] The exact origin of the term *Hibernia* is problematic, but it is probably strongly influenced by the common Latin adjective *hiberna* ("wintry, cold"), since the classical world originally viewed Ireland as a cold and wretched island, or at least as a land in the distant north.[31] The very similar name of the much-better-known Iberian peninsula, *Hiberia*, may have also played a role in the formation of the term *Hibernia*.

Caesar's information on Ireland probably derives from earlier Greek geographers, such as Pytheas, as well as direct inquiries of Gaulish and British natives. One can see this combination of sources later in the same chapter of the *Gallic War*, when he says that "some have written in the past" (*nonnulli scripserunt*) that in parts of the British Isles, the midwinter night lasts a full thirty days, but that he could confirm "nothing by inquiries" (*nihil de eo percontationibus*) once he arrived in Britain. Caesar relates that he did go to the trouble of determining by means of a water clock that nights in southern Britain were definitely shorter than those of Gaul. However, his invasion took him only a short way up the Thames, hundreds of kilometers from the western coast facing Ireland, so any measurement of distance between Britain and Ireland was second-hand information. But second-hand is not necessarily wrong. We know from his description of the Veneti tribe, who inhabited what is now southern Brittany, that these

Gaulish natives were excellent sailors who were skilled in the science of navigating and were accustomed to sailing regularly to Britain.[32] Caesar could have easily obtained information from the Veneti concerning the shores of southern Britain, and, given their skill, it is no great leap of the imagination to assume they were familiar with Irish waters as well.

Whatever his sources, the measurements Caesar reports are surprisingly accurate. Ireland is in fact approximately 82,460 square kilometers in area, not quite "less by half" of the 230,000 square kilometers of Britain "as it is estimated" by his sources, but not too far off in an age before precise measurements were possible. It is worth noting that a size comparison between the whole of Britain and Ireland also implies that Caesar's sources necessarily had at least a rough knowledge of the entire coastline of Ireland, not just the eastern coast facing Britain. Caesar's claim that the channel separating Britain from Ireland is equal to that dividing Britain and Gaul is also accurate, depending of course on where one chooses to measure. A straight passage from the Antrim coast of northern Ireland to the closest point on the Scottish coast is only about 22 kilometers, less than the roughly 33 kilometers between the cliffs of Dover and Calais in France. But it is likely that Caesar meant the similar width of the English Channel midway down the British coast compared to the distance across the Irish Sea at the Isle of Man (about 150 kilometers), since he says that Man (*Mona*) lies "midway" between Britain and Ireland, also a correct statement.[33]

Caesar's claim that the western side of Britain faces the Iberian peninsula with Ireland lying between the two is a mistake repeated by Pliny and Tacitus.[34] It was based on the faulty assumption that the western end of Britain lay opposite the Pyrenees mountains, which were thought to run north to south, separating Gaul from Spain. The error was rectified by the time of Ptolemy.[35]

Strabo

The geographer and historian Strabo (*c.* 64 B.C.–after A.D. 21) surveyed the ancient world in his monumental *Geography* (written c. A.D. 19), which ranged from the distant shores of India to Scythia, Africa, and, as he says, wretchedly cold Ireland in the northernmost region of the inhabitable world.[36] He was a Greek from Pontus in north-central Asia Minor, but his travels took him at least as far as Egypt and Italy, though he depends on earlier writers, such as Eratosthenes, much more than his own first-hand experience. Aside from Eratosthenes, his authorities include Pytheas, Posidonius, Hipparchus, Polybius, and many others, although he is seldom kind to his sources, especially Pytheas. Strabo's writings on Gaul and his few comments on Britain reveal that he was familiar with Caesar's *Gallic War*, but he directly refers to that commentary only once.[37] In general, his information on the islands off the coast of northwestern Europe is sketchy at best, while his placement of Ireland on the map of the inhabited world is gravely in error. His single, unflattering description of the Irish people themselves, though almost certainly without basis in fact, is important as the earliest unequivocal reference to the ethnography of Ireland. Strabo's *Geography* apparently remained largely unknown to scholars for almost two centuries after its completion. Later in the same century, Pliny, who mentions every conceivable source available to him, is silent concerning Strabo, as is Ptolemy in the mid-second century A.D. By the early third century, however, Strabo's *Geography* had gained a wider audience.

Strabo's references to Ireland begin with a defamation of Pytheas' reliability:[38]

ὅ τε γὰρ ἱστορῶν τὴν Θούλην Πυθέας ἀνὴρ ψευδίστατος ἐξήτασται, καὶ οἱ τὴν Βρεττανικὴν καὶ Ἰέρνην ἰδόντες οὐδὲν περὶ τῆς Θούλης λέγουσιν, ἄλλας νήσους λέγοντες μικρὰς περὶ τὴν Βρεττανικήν. (*Geography* 1.4.3)

For not only is the man who tells of Thule, Pytheas, shown to be the greatest of falsifiers, but those who have seen Britain and *Iernē* say nothing about Thule, speaking only of other small islands around Britain.

Pytheas describes Thule as the northernmost of the British Isles, lying on the Arctic Circle, a six-day sail from Britain, near a partially frozen sea.[39] This mysterious island has for two millennia been variously placed among the Orkney, Shetland, or Faroe island groups, or alternately identified as Iceland or Scandinavia.[40] Strabo does not believe in Thule's existence because it would be too far north to fit within his geographical framework. More importantly for our purposes, however, he refers to witnesses who had actually seen Britain, Ireland, and smaller islands of the British archipelago, but not Thule, to support his conclusions. Mention of these unknown sources is the earliest direct and certain reference we have for visitors to Ireland, or at least for travelers who sailed within sight of the island. The identity of these witnesses is unfortunately a mystery, but it is likely that merchants had been sailing to Ireland for centuries and that they are, via earlier writers, Strabo's ultimate source.[41] However, since merchants travel to make money, not to explore, it is probable that most would not have had occasion to sail to the desolate and unprofitable lands north of the British Isles where Thule supposedly lay.

Strabo is the first author to use the term * Iernē* ('Ιέρνη), the most common and long-lasting name for Ireland among the Greek authors, used until the end of the Roman empire. It is ultimately derived from the native Irish name either by direct contact with the Irish or through intermediaries such as the Gauls or British.

Shortly after his first passage on Ireland in the *Geography*, Strabo places Ireland on his world map in relation to Britain:

> ἀλλὰ μὴν ἐκ μέσης τῆς Βρεττανικῆς οὐ πλέον τῶν τετρακισχιλίων προε-
> λθὼν εὕροις ἂν οἰκήσιμον ἄλλως πως (τοῦτο δ' ἂν εἴη τὸ περὶ τὴν Ἰέρνην),
> ὥστε τὰ ἐπέκεινα, εἰς ἃ ἐκτοπίζει τὴν Θούλην, οὐκέτ' οἰκήσιμα. (*Geog-
> raphy* 1.4.4)

> But if you were to travel not more than 4,000 stadia [c. 800 kilometers[42]] north from the center of Britain, you would find a region only marginally habitable (this would be the region of *Iernē*), so that regions farther north, where Thule lies, are no longer habitable.

Exactly why Strabo mistakenly situates Ireland far to the north of Britain is uncertain. He was certainly aware of Caesar's *Gallic War*, which clearly places Ireland to the west of Britain, though Strabo throughout his work prefers Greek sources to Roman. However, no surviving Greek work of an earlier date specifically mentions the location of Ireland, though Eratosthenes, following Pytheas, sees Thule as an inhabited land north of Britain.[43] It is possible that Strabo, after dismissing the existence of Thule, felt the need to shift Ireland, which he knew to be inhabited, north of Britain in order to better fit his own theoretical framework and to place some European land on the northern margins of the inhabitable world, as he did on the southern margin with Ethiopia. Strabo was clearly following the tradition of earlier geographers in dividing the spherical world into arctic, temperate, and torrid zones. Only the temperate zones in both the northern and southern hemispheres were thought to be habitable. He placed Ireland at the uppermost border of the northern temperate zone, beyond which the climate was too cold for human habitation. Whatever Strabo's reasons

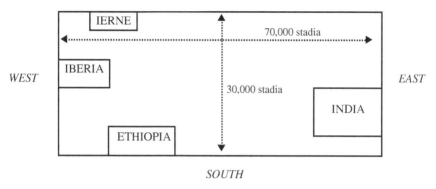

FIGURE 11. The Length and Width of the Inhabitable World in Strabo

for his positioning of Ireland, other writers had corrected his geographical and climatic mistakes by the end of the first century A.D.[44]

In Strabo's next statement on Ireland, he again notes that the island lies on the northernmost boundary of the inhabitable world:

διαμαρτὼν δὲ τοῦ πλάτους ἠνάγκασται καὶ τοῦ μήκους ἀστοχεῖν. ὅτι μὲν γὰρ πλέον ἢ διπλάσιον τὸ γνώριμον μῆκός ἐστι τοῦ γνωρίμου πλάτους, ὁμολογοῦσι καὶ οἱ ὕστερον καὶ τῶν παλαιῶν οἱ χαριέστατοι· λέγω δὲ τὸ ἀπὸ τῶν ἄκρων τῆς Ἰνδικῆς ἐπὶ τὰ ἄκρα τῆς Ἰβηρίας τοῦ ἀπ' Αἰθιόπων ἕως τοῦ κατὰ Ἰέρνην κύκλου. (*Geography* 1.4.5)

But since [Eratosthenes] misses entirely the width of the inhabitable world, he necessarily is mistaken as to the length as well. For more recent writers, as well as the best informed of the ancient scholars, agree that the known length is more than double the known width. I refer to the distance from the eastern end of India to the western edge of Iberia compared to the distance from Ethiopia to the parallel that runs through *Iernē*.

Strabo elsewhere gives the length of the known inhabitable world of the northern temperate zone as roughly 70,000 stadia (c. 14,000 kilometers) in length by 30,000 stadia (c. 6,000 kilometers) in width (see Fig. 11).[45] The actual distance from western Iberia to eastern India is roughly 10,000 kilometers, whereas the width of the latitude of Ireland to Ethiopia is approximately 5,000 kilometers. But the length of the whole Eurasian continent from Iberia to China, which Strabo was attempting to describe, is close to 14,000 kilometers. Thus we should credit Strabo with a remarkable degree of accuracy in his estimation given his limited knowledge of distant geography.

In Book Two of his *Geography*, Strabo describes the position of Ireland in relation to Celtica (Gaul) and comments again on the Irish climate:

> ὁ δέ γε ἀπὸ τῆς Κελτικῆς πρὸς ἄρκτον πλοῦς ἔσχατος λέγεται παρὰ τοῖς νῦν ὁ ἐπὶ τὴν Ἰέρνην, ἐπέκεινα μὲν οὖσαν τῆς Βρεττανικῆς, ἀθλίως δὲ διὰ ψῦχος οἰκουμένην, ὥστε τὰ ἐπέκεινα νομίζειν ἀοίκητα. οὐ πλέον δὲ τῆς Κελτικῆς τὴν Ἰέρνην διέχειν φασὶ τῶν πεντακισχιλίων. (*Geography* 2.1.13)

The voyage from Celtica to the north is currently said to be the most extreme. By this I mean the voyage beyond Britain to *Iernē*, a wretched place to live because of the cold, beyond which the lands are considered uninhabitable. They say that *Iernē* is separated from Celtica by not more than 5,000 stadia [c. 1,000 kilometers].

The actual distance from Gaul to Ireland is roughly 450 kilometers—half the figure Strabo gives.

Strabo continues his references to Ireland's position in a somewhat tedious discussion of the measurements of the northern temperate zone as given by the geographer Deimachus:

> ἡμεῖς δέ γε ἐπεδείκνυμεν μέχρι τῆς Ἰέρνης μόλις οἰκήσιμα ὄντα τὰ ὑπὲρ τὴν Κελτικήν, ἅπερ οὐ πλείω τῶν πεντακισχιλίων ἐστίν· οὗτος δ' ἀποφαίνει ὁ λόγος τῆς Ἰέρνης ἔτι βορειότερον εἶναί τινα κύκλον οἰκήσιμον σταδίοις τρισχιλίοις ὀκτακοσίοις . . . ταῦτα δὴ προστεθέντα τῷ ἀπὸ τῆς Ἰέρνης ἐπὶ τὰ βόρεια σταδιασμῷ ποιεῖ τὸ πᾶν διὰ τῆς ἀοικήτου διάστημα ἐπὶ τοῦ διὰ τῆς Ἰέρνης σταδιασμοῦ σταδίων ἑπτακισχιλίων καὶ ὀκτακοσίων· εἰ δὲ ἐάσειέ τις τοὺς τετρακισχιλίους σταδίους, αὐτά γε τὰ πρὸς τῷ Καυκάσῳ μέρη τῆς Βακτριανῆς ἔσται βορειότερα τῆς Ἰέρνης σταδίοις τρισχιλίοις καὶ ὀκτακοσίοις, τῆς δὲ Κελτικῆς καὶ τοῦ Βορυσθένους ὀκτακισχιλίοις καὶ ὀκτακοσίοις. (*Geography* 2.1.17)

I was explaining earlier how the regions beyond Celtica as far as *Iernē* are barely habitable, this distance being not more than 5,000 stadia

[1,000 kilometers]. However, this argument [of Deimachus] declares that there is a habitable latitude 3,800 stadia [760 kilometers] north beyond *Iernē*. . . . Adding these stadia to the figures from *Iernē* to the northern regions makes the total uninhabitable latitudes, beginning at the measurement through *Iernē*, 7,800 stadia [1,560 kilometers]. But if one omits these 4,000 stadia [800 kilometers], then at least the regions of Bactriana near the Caucasus will be 3,800 stadia [760 kilometers] farther north than *Iernē*, and 8,800 stadia [1,760 kilometers] north of Celtica and the Borysthenes.

We know little about Deimachus, aside from the fact he was an ambassador along with Megasthenes from the Hellenistic kingdom of Seleucus to an Indian ruler in the late fourth or early third century B.C. The meager fragments of his work deal primarily with India, but they also discuss the width of the inhabitable world.[46] Strabo here disagrees with the latitude Deimachus assigns to Bactriana in Asia near the Caucasus Mountains as it would mean abandoning his own theories and shifting the inhabitable zone much farther north than Ireland.

Strabo next expands his disagreements with previous geographers to include the reports of the second-century B.C. astronomer Hipparchus before returning to his criticism of Deimachus:

ἐν δὲ ταῖς χειμεριναῖς ἡμέραις ὁ ἥλιος μετεωρίζεται πήχεις ἕξ, τέτταρας δ' ἐν τοῖς ἀπέχουσι Μασσαλίας ἐνακισχιλίους σταδίους καὶ ἑκατόν, ἐλάττους δὲ τῶν τριῶν ἐν τοῖς ἐπέκεινα, οἳ κατὰ τὸν ἡμέτερον λόγον πολὺ ἂν εἶεν ἀρκτικώτεροι τῆς Ἰέρνης . . . εἴρηται γὰρ ὅτι κατὰ τοὺς περὶ Δήμαχον συμβήσεται βορειοτέρους εἶναι τῆς Ἰέρνης τοὺς πρὸς τῷ Καυκάσῳ Βακτρίους σταδίοις τρισχιλίοις ὀκτακοσίοις· προστεθέντων δὲ τούτων τοῖς ἀπὸ Μασσαλίας εἰς Ἰέρνην, γίνονται μύριοι δισχίλιοι πεντακόσιοι. (*Geography* 2.1.18)

Hipparchus reports that in the regions 6,300 stadia [1,260 kilometers] from Massalia the sun only rises six cubits [12 degrees][47] on winter days, and in the lands 9,100 stadia [1,820 kilometers] from Massalia, only four cubits [8 degrees], and less than three cubits [6 degrees] in the regions of the supposed people beyond (who, according to my argument, would be much farther north than *Iernē*). . . . I have said that according to the followers of Deimachus, the Bactrians living near the Caucasus are 3,800 stadia [760 kilometers] farther north than *Ierne*. Adding this distance to that from Massalia to *Ierne* yields a total of 12,500 stadia [2,500 kilometers].

Though Hipparchus was considered the greatest of the ancient astronomers and the first to systematically apply rigorous mathematical standards to geography, Strabo has no difficulty in disagreeing with him where Hipparchus' measurements contradict his own.

Strabo subsequently returns to his theme of Ireland's northern location and comments on the character of its inhabitants:

νομίζω δὲ πολὺ εἶναι νοτιώτερον τούτου τὸ τῆς οἰκουμένης πέρας τὸ προσάρκτιον· οἱ γὰρ νῦν ἱστοροῦντες περαιτέρω τῆς Ἰέρνης οὐδὲν ἔχουσι λέγειν, ἢ πρὸς ἄρκτον πρόκειται τῆς Βρεττανικῆς πλησίον, ἀγρίων τελέως ἀνθρώπων καὶ κακῶς οἰκούντων διὰ ψύχος, ὥστ᾽ ἐνταῦθα νομίζω τὸ πέρας εἶναι θετέον. . .τὸ δ᾽ ἐκεῖθεν ἐπὶ τὴν Ἰέρνην οὐκέτι γνώριμον, πόσον ἄν τις θείη, οὐδ᾽ εἰ περαιτέρω ἔτι οἰκήσιμά ἐστιν, οὐδὲ δεῖ φροντίζειν τοῖς ἐπάνω λεχθεῖσι προέχοντας. (*Geography* 2.5.8)

But I think that the limit of the inhabitable world is much farther south than this. For modern researchers have nothing to say on lands beyond *Ierne*, which lies near Britain to its north, where completely wild people live a wretched existence on account of the cold. This place, I believe, is the limit of the habitable world. . . . But the distance one should set down from Britain to *Ierne* is no longer known, nor if there are habitable regions beyond, nor is it necessary to consider the problem if we believe the above arguments.

Before this passage begins, Strabo has related that Pytheas placed the inhabited island of Thule at the Arctic Circle, 66 degrees north latitude, a location that would fit either Iceland or Scandinavia. But Strabo believes instead that Ireland is the northernmost inhabitable land in the world and lies south of this line. As earlier he appealed to the lack of sightings of Thule by those who sailed to Britain and Ireland as evidence that Thule was a figment of Pytheas' imagination, he here appeals to its absence in the writings of "modern researchers" (ἱστοροῦντες). Strabo previously had deduced that any land as cold as he believed Ireland to be would also be a miserable place to live, but here he adds that the freezing climate of the island has made the inhabitants complete savages. This view, which in his final passage he admits is pure speculation, simply follows a prejudicial tradition against marginal peoples stretching from Homer to modern times.

Strabo concludes this section by referring to his earlier statement that the distance from Britain to Ireland is 4,000 stadia (800 kilometers), declaring here the distance is unknown, though a few lines after this passage he says 3,000 to 4,000 stadia is the likely distance.

In the next two passages, Strabo returns to his conviction that Ireland defines the uppermost limit of habitable lands:

> ἔστι δή τι χλαμυδοειδὲς σχῆμα τῆς γῆς τῆς οἰκουμένης, οὗ τὸ μὲν πλάτος ὑπογράφει τὸ μέγιστον ἡ διὰ τοῦ Νείλου γραμμή, λαβοῦσα τὴν ἀρχὴν ἀπὸ τοῦ διὰ τῆς Κινναμωμοφόρου παραλλήλου καὶ τῆς τῶν Αἰγυπτίων τῶν φυγάδων νήσου μέχρι τοῦ διὰ τῆς Ἰέρνης παραλλήλου. (*Geography* 2.5.14)

The shape of the inhabitable world is somewhat like a *chlamys*, whose greatest width is a line through the Nile, which begins at the parallel running through the cinnamon-producing land and the isle of the Egyptian refugees and ends at the parallel through *Iernē*.

> ὁ δὲ γεωγράφος ἐπισκοπεῖ ταύτην μόνην τὴν καθ' ἡμᾶς οἰκουμένην. αὕτη δ' ἀφορίζεται πέρασι νοτίῳ μὲν τῷ διὰ τῆς Κινναμωμοφόρου παραλλήλῳ, βορείῳ δὲ τῷ διὰ Ἰέρνης. (*Geography* 2.5.34)

The geographer examines only our inhabited world. This is defined in the south by the parallel passing through the cinnamon-producing lands and in the north by the parallel through *Iernē*.

A *chlamys* is a short cloak often worn by a horseman that was fastened on the shoulder by a brooch. Strabo saw the northern lands as relatively narrow, spreading out like a cloak as one moved south to Africa and India. On the southern border of this cloak, at the opposite extreme from Ireland, were the *Sembritae*, deserters and refugees from the Egyptian army who in the seventh century B.C. had settled on an island in the southern Nile.[48] On the same latitude were the regions on the African horn south of Arabia that produce cinnamon.

Strabo's final statement on Ireland is in many ways the most interesting, as it deals not so much with geography as with the supposed character of the Irish natives:

> εἰσὶ δὲ καὶ ἄλλαι περὶ τὴν Βρεττανικὴν νῆσοι μικραί· μεγάλη δ' ἡ Ἰέρνη πρὸς ἄρκτον αὐτῇ παραβεβλημένη πρόμηκες μᾶλλον πλάτος ἔχουσα. περὶ ἧς οὐδὲν ἔχομεν λέγειν σαφές, πλὴν ὅτι ἀγριώτεροι τῶν Βρεττανῶν ὑπάρ-

χουσιν οἱ κατοικοῦντες αὐτήν, ἀνθρωποφάγοι τε ὄντες καὶ πολυφάγοι,
τούς τε πατέρας τελευτήσαντας κατεσθίειν ἐν καλῷ τιθέμενοι καὶ φανερῶς
μίσγεσθαι ταῖς τε ἄλλαις γυναιξὶ καὶ μητράσι καὶ ἀδελφαῖς· καὶ ταῦτα δ᾽
οὕτω λέγομεν, ὡς οὐκ ἔχοντες ἀξιοπίστους μάρτυρας, καίτοι τό γε τῆς
ἀνθρωποφαγίας καὶ Σκυθικὸν εἶναι λέγεται, καὶ ἐν ἀνάγκαις πολιορκητι-
καῖς καὶ Κελτοὶ καὶ Ἴβηρες καὶ ἄλλοι πλείους ποιῆσαι τοῦτο λέγονται.
(*Geography* 4.5.4)

There are also other smaller islands around Britain, the largest being *Iernē*, which lies to its north and is longer than it is wide. Concerning this island I have nothing certain to report, except that the people living there are more savage than the Britons, being cannibals as well as gluttons. Further, they consider it honorable to eat their dead fathers and to openly have intercourse, not only with unrelated women, but with their mothers and sisters as well. I say these things not having trustworthy witnesses, and yet the custom of cannibalism is said to be found among the Scythians, and, because of necessity during sieges, the Celts, Iberians, and others besides are said to have practiced it.

Strabo is the first writer to comment on the shape of Ireland, al-though Caesar several decades earlier related that its size was roughly half that of Britain.[49] Strabo is certainly correct in his claim that Ireland is longer in one direction than in the other, but unfortunately he gives no di-mensions for the island, as later writers do. Although there has been some uncertainty as to whether Strabo claims Ireland is longer in an east-west or a north-south direction (as it really is), it seems best to read this passage as indicating that the east-west axis of Ireland is the greater in length.[50] It seems strange that Strabo (or his sources) not only put Ireland far to the north of Britain but reversed its orientation as well, almost as if he had taken the true axis and position of the island and moved it 90 degrees clockwise on his map (see Fig. 12).

The remainder of this last passage is devoted to a standard classical portrayal of remote barbarian cultures, for which Strabo at least admits he has neither certainty nor trustworthy sources. The charge of Irish canni-balism is found previously in Diodorus Siculus, assuming Diodorus was referring to Ireland.[51] Greek and Roman sources routinely accused distant tribes of eating human flesh, but Strabo here is plainly inspired by Herodo-tus' dubious claim that the Indian Callatiae, the Issedones of Scythia, and

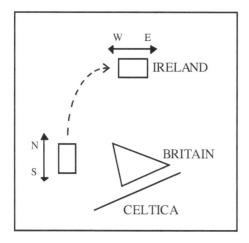

FIGURE 12. The Possible Shift of Ireland in a
Clockwise Direction by Strabo

the Massagetae consumed their dead fathers in ritual cannibalism.[52] It is
interesting to note that Strabo assumes cannibalism among the Irish based
partially on the reports of the same activity among the Scythians, whom
he also places on the extreme northern border of the habitable lands.[53] He
then attempts to make his unfounded accusations of man-eating more pal-
atable by noting that even those cultures closer to the civilizing influence
of the Mediterranean world would resort to cannibalism in cases of siege
during war.[54] Gluttony was also a common feature associated with barbarians, while the accusations of promiscuity and incest may have been inspired
by reports such as those of Caesar (on the Britons) or Herodotus (on various cultures) concerning group marriages and licentious behavior.[55] The
charges of cannibalism and incest are almost identical to those later levied
against the early Christians by their enemies.[56]

Isidorus

Very little is known of the geographer Isidorus except that he was a Greek
from Charax in southern Mesopotamia who lived during the reign of Augustus (early first century A.D.). His only complete work, the *Parthian Sta-
tions*, describes a journey from the Mediterranean to India. One isolated
passage generally attributed to Isidorus briefly discusses the size of vari-

ous large islands in the Mediterranean and Atlantic, including Britain and Ireland:

τῶν δὲ Βρεττανικῶν νήσων ἡ μεγίστη καλουμένη Ἀλβίων τὴν περίμετρον ἔχει σταδίων τρισμυρίων ἐννακισχιλίων, ἡ δὲ Ἰέρνη ἀναλόγως ταύτης μείζων. (*Geographi Graeci Minores* 2.509)

The greatest of the Brettanic Isles, which is called *Albion*, has a circumference of 39,000 stadia [7,800 kilometers], but *Iernē* in comparison is larger.

If the manuscript is correct, Isidorus is unique among ancient geographers in claiming that Ireland is larger than Britain. But it may be that the word μείζων ("larger") is a textual corruption of an original μείων ("smaller") by the simple addition of a single Greek letter (ζ), so that the original reading would be "but *Iernē* in comparison is *smaller*." Regardless of his accuracy as to Ireland, Isidorus makes Britain more than twice as large as Caesar's 2,000 Roman miles (2,960 kilometers) in circumference.[57]

Pomponius Mela

Pomponius Mela, born near Gibraltar in southern Spain, wrote the first surviving Latin geographical work, *De chorographia* (*On Geography*, c. A.D. 44), at roughly the same time the Romans under Claudius were invading and occupying southern Britain. In this book he briefly describes the whole of the known world, including Africa, Asia, the Mediterranean, Gaul, and the British Isles. Like Herodotus, however, he focuses more on ethnography, wonders, and mythological stories than on precise mathematical geography. Mela's short description of Ireland includes comments on its size, climate, agriculture, and the character of the inhabitants:[58]

super Britanniam Iuverna est paene par spatio, sed utrimque aequali tractu litorum oblonga, caeli ad maturanda semina iniqui, verum adeo luxuriosa herbis non laetis modo sed etiam dulcibus, ut se exigua parte diei pecora implent, et nisi pabulo prohibeantur, diutius pasta dissiliant. cultores eius inconditi sunt, et omnium virtutum ignari magis quam aliae gentes, pietatis admodum expertes. (*De chorographia* 3.53)

Beyond Britain is *Iuverna*, almost the same in area, but oblong with coasts of equal length on both sides. The climate is unfavorable for the ripening of grain, but yet it is so fertile for grass, not only abundant but sweet, that livestock eat their fill in a small part of the day. Unless they were restrained from this pasturage, they would burst from feeding too long. The inhabitants of this island are unrefined, ignorant of all the virtues more than any other people, and totally lacking all sense of duty.

Mela says that Ireland is *super Britanniam*, meaning either "above Britain," in the same sense that Strabo places Ireland to the north, or simply "beyond Britain," from the point of view of a Mediterranean writer. Perhaps Mela himself did not have a clear picture of Ireland's location other than a vague idea that it lay somewhere on the far side of Britain, though if he is following Greek sources it is likely he places Ireland to the north. Regardless of its exact position, Mela believes that Ireland and Britain are of roughly equal size, unlike Caesar, who says the island is only half as big as Britain, and Isidorus, who perhaps sees it as even larger.[59] Mela follows the same, generally accurate tradition as Strabo in saying that Ireland is rectangular in shape (*oblongus*), with parallel coasts of equal length, though again like Strabo he does not provide dimensions, nor does he say whether the longer axis is north-south or east-west.[60] Mela's use of the name *Iuverna* for Ireland rather than Caesar's *Hibernia* further suggests his dependence on Greek rather than Latin sources.[61]

Unlike Strabo, Mela felt no need to prove that Ireland lay on the northern edge of the habitable world, and at least allowed Ireland to be abundantly rich in grass if not in grain — indeed, so abundant that the fear of exploding cattle would ever be in the mind of a worried Irish herdsman. This dire result of the gases produced by overgrazing actually has a basis in fact, according to modern farmers. Intriguingly, the same danger was also reported a generation earlier by Pompeius Trogus (via the *Epitome* of Justin) of the mythological cattle of Geryon in a region of Spain "made up of islands" (*ex insulis constat*), perhaps a garbled reference to the British Isles or a common tradition adapted by Mela.[62] In addition, the Roman historian Curtius soon after Mela has a very similar account when he describes pastoralism in the rich lands of Mesopotamia.[63] Mela does not give his source, if any, for his information on the character of the Irish people. He does not accuse the Irish of cannibalism, unlike Strabo and perhaps Diodorus, but to say they are unrefined, most ignorant of virtue, and lacking in all *pietas* seems in many ways more harsh.[64] This condemnation of the Irish is much worse than his description of the British just previous to this passage as merely *inculti* ("uncivilized, unpolished") and may simply reflect a prejudice that any people lying beyond the British in location must necessarily surpass them in vice as well.[65]

Pliny the Elder

Gaius Plinius Secundus (better known as Pliny the Elder, as he was the uncle of the famed correspondent Pliny the Younger) was born in Cisalpine Gaul around A.D. 23/4, served as a respected military leader in Germany and Spain, and perished while investigating the eruption of Vesuvius in A.D. 79. Pliny is best known for his monumental and all-encompassing *Natural History* (written c. A.D. 77), an encyclopedia of contemporary knowledge in the mid-first-century A.D. Roman world covering every imaginable topic from agriculture, art, and warfare to geography and ethnography. He claims to have consulted over two thousand sources while researching his voluminous work, and he cites numerous authors, both well and poorly known.[66] Pliny mentions Ireland only in one brief passage focusing on Britain and the lands of the northwest Atlantic:

> *xxx prope iam annis notitiam eius Romanis armis*
> *non ultra vicinitatem silvae Calidoniae*
> *propagantibus. Agrippa longitudinem DCCC esse*
> *latitudinem CCC credit, eandem Hiberniae, sed*
> *longitudinem CC minorem. super eam haec sita*
> *abest brevissimo transitu a Silurum gente XXX.*
> *reliquarum nulla CXXV amplior circuitu proditur.*
> *sunt autem XL Orcades modicis inter se discretae*
> *spatiis, VII Acmodae, XXX Hebudes, et inter*
> *Hiberniam ac Britanniam Mona, Monapia, Riginia,*
> *Vectis, Silumnus, Andros. (Natural History 4.102–3)*

Almost thirty years ago, Britain was explored by Roman armies to the area not beyond the Calidonian forest. Agrippa believes the longitude of the island to be 800 miles [1,184 kilometers] and the latitude 300 miles [444 kilometers], and *Hibernia* the same latitude but 200 miles [296 kilometers] less in longitude. *Hibernia* lies beyond Britain with the shortest crossing being from the Silures tribe at 30 miles [44 kilometers]. It is said that none of the remaining islands

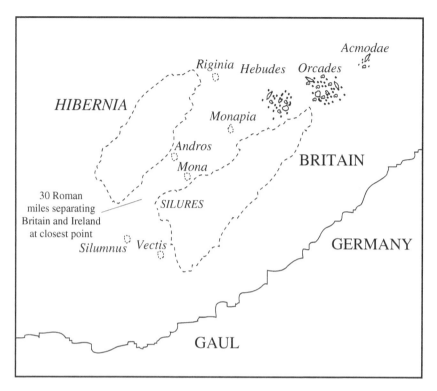

FIGURE 13. The Position of Ireland and Nearby Islands in Pliny
(*Many Sizes and Locations Conjectural*)

has a circumference of more than 125 miles [185 kilometers]. There are forty *Orcades* separated from each other by small distances, seven *Acmodae*, thirty *Hebudes*, and between *Hibernia* and Britain are *Mona*, *Monapia*, *Riginia*, *Vectis*, *Silumnus*, and *Andros* (see Fig. 13).

Although Pliny is writing more than thirty years after the Roman invasion and occupation of southern Britain under Claudius, his knowledge of Britain, not to mention Ireland, is still quite vague and incomplete. After Julius Caesar's brief forays into southeastern Britain in 55 and 54 B.C., there was a ninety-one-year absence of Roman power on the island. In A.D. 43, the Roman armies landed in Britain and began a slow conquest of the southern regions that continued until the governorship of Agricola. Roman forces under Agricola completed the pacification of Wales and invaded northern Britain in A.D. 79, just after the time Pliny wrote his *Natural History*.

Pliny is never reluctant to reveal his sources for a subject, with the geography of Britain and Ireland fortunately no exception. He lists Pytheas, Isidorus, Timaeus, and Agrippa as sources on Britain, and Agrippa specifically in this passage for the dimensions of Ireland. Marcus Vipsanius Agrippa (c. 64–12 B.C.) was the trusted supporter, general, and friend of the emperor Augustus who undertook an official geographical study of the empire and regions beyond for his patron. His geographical commentary, based largely on earlier Greek sources, was even used in the creation of a world map on public display in Rome after his death. Pliny also lists many other sources for Europe and western Asia that may have contributed to his survey of the British Isles, including Eratosthenes, Ephorus, Polybius, Posidonius, Pomponius Mela, and Philemon.[67] Though Pliny does not directly cite him in his section on Ireland, the little-known merchant and geographer Philemon, who wrote earlier in the first century A.D., is potentially the most interesting of Pliny's sources for this passage. For we know, according to Ptolemy, that Philemon received information directly from merchants who had traveled to Ireland.[68]

Pliny is the first ancient author to give dimensions for Ireland, though earlier writers had discussed its size relative to Britain and even the circumference of the island. According to Pliny, the *latitudo* of Ireland is 300 Roman miles (444 kilometers), the same as Britain's, and the *longitudo* is 600 miles (888 kilometers), 200 miles less than Britain's.[69] Taking these two terms at face value as "latitude" (north-south width) and "longitude" (east-west length) would make both Britain and Ireland much longer in an east-west dimension than they are north-south, the opposite of what is indeed the case, though firmly in the tradition of Strabo and his Greek sources.[70]

Unfortunately, like Pomponius Mela before him, Pliny says only that Ireland is *super* Britain without clearly indicating if he means the island is simply "beyond" or somewhere "to the north of" Britain. Since Pliny is writing more than thirty years after the Roman occupation of southern Britain, we might reasonably assume he should know better than to orient Britain, and even Ireland, with the longer axis east-west rather than north-south. However, Pliny uses *latitudo* and *longitudo* many times throughout his *Natural History* and clearly intends the reader to always understand a north-south and an east-west orientation, respectively, though not necessarily directly north-south or east-west.[71]

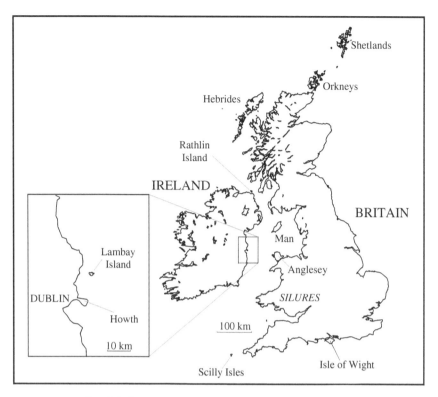

FIGURE 14. Possible Locations Mentioned by Pliny

The shortest distance between Britain and Ireland, according to Pliny, is the 30 Roman miles (44 kilometers) between the coast of Ireland and the British Silures tribe. The *Silures* lived in southeastern Wales near present-day Cardiff, but the *Demetae* tribe lived on the Welsh coast to their west and were thus closer to Ireland, as were the *Ordovices* and *Deceangli* of northern Wales and the *Novantae* and *Epidii* of southwestern Scotland. Actually, the shortest distance between Britain and Ireland is the roughly 22 kilometers from the Kintyre peninsula in Scotland to the Antrim coast in northern Ireland. The shortest distance between Wales and Ireland is approximately 75 kilometers from St. David's Head in southern Wales to Carnsore Point in southeast Ireland. The *Silures* tribe in southeast Wales was almost 200 kilometers distant from Ireland (see Fig. 14).

Pliny lists a number of islands near Britain and Ireland, but unfortunately he does not describe their locations except for the six he simply describes as "between Ireland and Britain" (*inter Hiberniam ac Britanniam*). In several cases, the best we can do is try to match them to islands listed seventy-five years later by Ptolemy, who does give locations, or to match them to names and locations in other authors. Pliny states that there are forty *Orcades* islands near Britain, which can be no other than the Orkney Islands just off the northern Scottish coast (see Fig. 14).[72] The seven *Acmodae* are more difficult to identify precisely, but they are probably the Shetland Islands to the northeast of the Orkneys.[73] Pliny's thirty *Hebudes* must be the Hebrides, just off Scotland's northwest coast.[74] The islands that Pliny describes as lying between Ireland and Britain, such as *Mona*, present more difficulties in identification. Caesar says that *Mona* is located midway (*medio cursu*) between Britain and Ireland, which fits the Isle of Man very well.[75] Ptolemy also places *Mona* (*Μόνα*) midway in the Irish Sea, which argues for Man, though he frequently places islands too far off a coast.[76] Tacitus, on the other hand, is very clear that *Mona* is Anglesey (Welsh *Môn*), which is separated from the northwest Welsh coast only by a narrow channel that the Roman army waded across to destroy a druid stronghold.[77] Pliny complicates the matter by saying that *Monapia* also lies between Britain and Ireland. *Monapia*, which may be the same as Ptolemy's *Monaoida* (*Μονάοιδα*), is also identified with the Isle of Man in the classical tradition.[78] Pliny's *Riginia*, which Ptolemy calls *Rhikina* (*Ῥικίνα*) and places off the northeast coast of Ireland, may be Rathlin Island in the channel between Scotland and Ireland.[79] The island of *Vectis* is almost certainly the Isle of Wight, which is not between Ireland and Britain at all, but just off the southern British coast.[80] *Silumnus* may be one of the Scilly Isles off the western coast of Cornwall (almost in the Irish Sea), while *Andros* might possibly be Howth or Lambay near Dublin Bay.[81]

Perhaps more important than the precise identification of individual islands with their modern counterparts is what the report of these islands by Pliny tells us about how relations between Ireland and the classical world improved from the first century B.C. to the first century A.D. In the mid-first century B.C., Caesar had only a vague idea that Ireland lay beyond the island of *Mona* to the west of Britain and was roughly half as large.[82] Strabo knew of some small islands "around Britain" in the early first century A.D., but did not name them or say they were near Ireland.[83] Even at the time of the Roman conquest of southern Britain in 44 A.D., Pomponius Mela mentioned only the *Orcades* and *Acmodae* off Britain's northern coast.[84] But by the time Pliny is writing, around 77 A.D., the Romans knew of at least nine islands or island groups besides Ireland and Britain in the British Isles. Granted, Pliny may have misplaced *Vectis* (Isle of Wight) when he said it was between Ireland and Britain, but if the above identifications are correct, the other islands he identifies as *inter* ("between") *Hiberniam ac Britanniam* really do lie between the two. Especially worth noting are *Andros* and *Riginia*. Whether *Andros* is Lambay, Howth, or some other nearby location, a number of Roman artifacts from the first century A.D. have been found in the area of Dublin Bay, as have artifacts dating from the second century A.D. at Rathlin Island and its vicinity. The knowledge of island names in Pliny surely reflects an increase in merchant traffic between Ireland and the Roman world at this time. Such statements as those of Tacitus on the knowledge of approaches and harbors in Ireland due to trade, and of Ptolemy on Philemon, who gathered reports from merchants trading with Ireland in the first century A.D., help to explain the advances in Irish geography found in Pliny.[85]

Pseudo-Aristotle

A number of works in antiquity are spuriously attributed to the philosopher Aristotle (384–322 B.C.), including a short survey of the world known as *De mundo* (On the Cosmos). This short but influential text may have been composed anytime from the mid-first century B.C. to the end of the first century A.D.

After noting a number of large islands in the Mediterranean, such as Sicily and Crete, the author moves on to the isles of the Atlantic:

> ἐν τούτῳ γε μὴν νῆσοι μέγισται τυγχάνουσιν οὖσαι δύο, Βρεττανικαὶ λεγόμεναι, Ἀλβίων καὶ Ἰέρνη, τῶν προϊστορημένων μείζους, ὑπὲρ τοὺς Κελτοὺς κείμεναι. (*De mundo* 3.393b [Lorimer 1933])

> In this Ocean lie two large islands, called the Brettanic Isles, Albion and *Iernē*, larger than those mentioned above, lying above the Celts.

The author of *De mundo* follows the earlier tradition of grouping together Ireland and Britain as the Brettanic Isles, using the older name *Albion* for Britain in this pairing, as does Isidorus.[86] But this unknown geographer does not give any figures for the sizes or shapes of the two islands, nor does he report their locations relative to each other.

Tacitus

Cornelius Tacitus (c. 56–after 118 A.D.) was born in Cisalpine or Narbonese Gaul and later rose to positions of power in Roman government under the emperors Vespasian, Titus, and Domitian. His rise was certainly aided by marriage to the daughter of Gnaeus Julius Agricola, governor of Britain from A.D. 77 to 84. Tacitus' works of Roman history include the *Agricola* (c. A.D. 98), a biography of his father-in-law, as well as the *Germania, Dialogue, Histories,* and *Annals* (c. A.D. 118). Of his two passages on Ireland, one is merely a passing reference in the *Annals,* but the other—a discussion of the island in the *Agricola*—is one of the most important and informative passages on Ireland in classical literature.

After four campaign seasons, Agricola had subdued the British tribes from northern Wales to southern Scotland. The fifth season (A.D. 82) saw the movement of his legions into the regions just north of the Solway Firth:

> *quinto expeditionum anno nave prima transgressus ignotas ad id tempus gentes crebris simul ac prosperis proeliis domuit; eamque partem Britanniae quae Hiberniam aspicit copiis instruxit, in spem magis quam ob formidinem, si quidem Hibernia medio inter Britanniam atque Hispaniam sita et Gallico quoque mari opportuna valentissimam imperii partem magnis in vicem usibus miscuerit. spatium eius, si Britanniae comparetur, angustius, nostri maris insulas superat. solum caelumque et ingenia cultusque hominum haud multum a Britannia differunt; [in melius] aditus portusque per commercia et negotiatores cognoti. Agricola expulsum seditione domestica unum ex regulis gentis exceperat ac specie amicitiae in occasionem retinebat. saepe ex eo audivi legione una et modicis auxiliis debellari obtinerique Hiberniam posse; idque etiam adversus Britanniam profuturum, si Romana ubique arma et velut e conspectu libertas tolleretur.* (*Agricola* 24)

In the fifth year of the war, Agricola, crossing in the lead ship, conquered tribes unknown until that time in frequent and successful engagements. That part of Britain which faces *Hibernia* he garrisoned with troops, more out of hope than out of fear. For *Hibernia,* lying between Britain and Hispania, and placed strategically in the Gallic Sea, would unite the most robust parts of the empire to the great advantage of both. In size it surpasses the islands of our sea, but it is narrower than Britain. As for soil, climate, and the character and

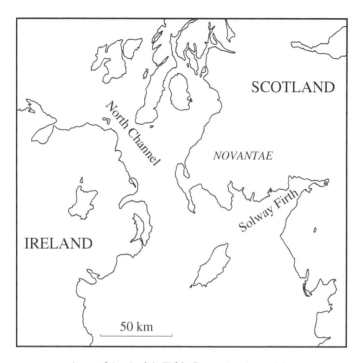

FIGURE 15. Area of Agricola's Fifth Campaign (A.D. 82)

lifestyle of its people, it differs little from Britain. The approaches and harbors are [better] known due to trade and merchants. Agricola had taken in one of their tribal kings driven out by an internal discord and was keeping him under the pretense of friendship for the right opportunity. I often heard him say that *Hibernia* could be conquered and occupied by one legion and a moderate number of auxiliaries. Moreover, it would be useful against Britain as well if Roman arms were everywhere raised high and liberty, so to speak, vanished from sight.

Agricola began this campaign by himself sailing in the lead ship across an unspecified body of water (probably the Solway Firth) into the land of the *Novantae* tribe just across the narrow North Channel from Ireland (see Fig. 15). The distance between Britain and Ireland at this point is only about 22 kilometers, with an unimpeded view of the hills of Ulster from the Scottish coast. No doubt Agricola looked on these hills as he

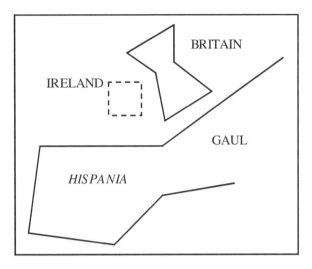

FIGURE 16. Ireland's Position between Britain and Spain
According to Tacitus

dreamed of a campaign against the Irish; perhaps he even sent across a
scouting expedition or two to the island, though no record of such exploration remains. The troops he stationed in the land of the Novantae facing
Ireland were necessary for maintaining control of that area of Scotland,
but they also would have been useful for any future Irish operations.

But why did Agricola want to invade Ireland? The Romans did not
generally conquer lands unless there were strategic or financial reasons to
do so. Armies were and are expensive to maintain, so that any conquest
ideally had to at least recoup its cost by means of plunder or tribute. Earlier
in the first century A.D., Strabo had argued that there was nothing to be
gained from controlling Britain and the islands to the north (where he
placed Ireland), as the inhabitants could neither benefit nor injure Rome.[87]
But by the time of Agricola, Britain had been added to the empire, so that
Ireland stood out as one of the few sizable territories remaining in western
Europe that was not under Roman control. Tacitus does not attribute economic motivations to Agricola, even though Ireland had at least enough
goods to justify the visits of Roman traders; rather, he ascribes strategic
and psychological reasons for Ireland's subjugation. This is partially due to
the idea, still uncorrected in Tacitus' day, that Ireland lay midway between
Britain and Spain (*medio inter Britanniam atque Hispaniam*) (see Fig. 16).[88]

Seen from this perspective, Ireland would indeed have served as a useful link between Britain and the Iberian peninsula. Its subjugation would also, as Tacitus notes at the end of this passage, have eliminated the troublesome example of a free land from the view of potential rebels in nearby Britain.

Tacitus continues the tradition of earlier writers who report that Ireland is smaller than Britain. He sounds very much like the pseudo-Aristotelian author of the *De mundo* when he says that Ireland is larger than the islands of the Mediterranean Sea, but he does not give any figures for the size of Ireland, nor does he comment on its shape.[89] He does, however, return to Caesar's correct placement of Ireland to the west, not to the north, of Britain.[90] The climate and soil of Ireland in his opinion are quite similar to Britain's, which he elsewhere describes as rainy and damp, but not too cold, and excellent for growing crops aside from olives and grapevines.[91]

Even more interesting is Tacitus' statement that the Irish people were very similar to the British in character and culture. We must be careful not to read too much into such a general comparison, but in the same work Tacitus depicts the British as having a tribal and warlike society divided by class into the nobility and their dependents.[92] Modern archaeological evidence supports this similarity between the British and Irish in respect to material culture, and comparative studies in religion, mythology, and social structure find many common points between Britain and Ireland that can be traced to at least the Roman era.[93] Tacitus also finds close similarities between the British and the Gauls in religion and language, but he omits any specific religious or linguistic references in his comparison of Irish and British culture.[94] This does not necessarily mean that Irish religion and language differed markedly from those of the British; in fact, the evidence suggests that at least the gods and rituals of Ireland were quite similar to those of Britain. The limited linguistic evidence does suggest that the British and Gaulish languages were very similar at this time, but although both British and Irish derived from a common linguistic source, the relationship between those two languages was probably not as close as that between British and Gaulish.

Tacitus then makes the surprising statement that the approaches and harbors (*aditus portusque*) of Ireland are better known than those of Britain.[95] As the Romans had actually occupied southern Britain for several decades, whereas they had only traded with Ireland, this seems unlikely. The phrase "better known" probably is simply a later addition to the origi-

BRITAIN

IRELAND

☐ Roman-occupied Britain
before Agricola

100 km

• Sites with Roman artifacts
in Ireland (1st cent. A.D.)

FIGURE 17. Agricola's Campaigns in Britain (A.D. 74–84)

nal manuscript.[96] Regardless of Tacitus' exact meaning, the crucial point of this section is that merchants from Roman lands were visiting Ireland. This is confirmed by numerous Roman archaeological finds in Ireland dating from the first century A.D. (see Fig. 17) and by the corroborative statement of Ptolemy concerning merchants in Ireland at this time.[97] A faint recollection of outside trade at this period may even be preserved in medieval Irish writings, as the twelfth-century *Metrical Dindshenchas*, a poetic account of place-name origins, says there was once gold and fine clothing available at a great market of the "Greek Gauls" or "Greek foreigners" at an ancient town called *Carmun*.[98]

The nameless *regulus* ("petty king, chieftain") noted next by Tacitus in the retinue of Agricola is the first (and possibly the only) individual Irish person mentioned in classical literature.[99] The warm acceptance of disgruntled foreign rulers for possible future use is found throughout Greek and Roman history, from the numerous Greek kings and political leaders seeking refuge at the Persian court to the British rulers who fled to the early Roman emperors.[100] Medieval Irish literature is also full of exiled nobility fleeing to the enemy camp. Fergus Mac Roich, former king of Ulster, fled to the capital of Ailill and Medb in western Ireland when betrayed by the new king Conchobar. He then joined his former enemies in the famous cattle raid on Ulster celebrated in the *Táin Bó Cúailgne*. His flight was prompted by treacherous events after the return of other exiles, Deirdre and the Sons of Uisnech, from Scotland, where they had fled. In fact, Britain seems a favorite refuge for disgruntled Irish nobility in medieval tales set in pre-Christian times, including the stories of Tuathal Techmar and Da Derga's hostel (*Togail Bruidne Da Derga*). Attempts have been made to identify Agricola's Irish *regulus* with characters in medieval Irish tales.[101] Though these efforts are intriguing, it is always a risky business to match figures from mythology to those from history, even when the myths may have a historical basis. One fact we can safely deduce from the presence of an Irish nobleman in a Roman camp is bilingualism. Somehow this Irish king communicated with Agricola, whether the *regulus* himself knew Latin or a translator spoke for him. It should not be surprising that some foreigners knew the Irish language, or that Irish merchants themselves may have been familiar with British, Gaulish, or Latin, as trade could hardly have been carried on in Ireland without some ability to communicate.

The claim of an experienced general like Agricola that Ireland could be taken and occupied by one legion and a moderate number of auxiliaries should be taken seriously.[102] A Roman legion in the first century A.D. contained between 5,000 and 6,000 soldiers, whereas auxiliary groups of infantry and cavalry numbered anywhere from 500 to 1,000 soldiers. Southern Britain was conquered by four legions and their auxiliaries in the mid-first century A.D., and a similar number of troops held the island and expanded Roman control into northern Britain under Agricola. Ireland is not considerably larger than the area of Britain under Roman dominion before Agricola's governorship, so one may wonder why the invasion would require only a quarter of the number of troops needed in the southern British conquest. Perhaps Agricola felt the resistance would be less organized or less formidable in Ireland than it had been in Britain, or perhaps he calculated that his experienced Roman troops, who had conquered many of the tribes of central and northern Britain in eight years, were better prepared for war against the Irish. Given the almost universal inability of the ancient Celts to cooperate in defense against the Romans, it is likely that Agricola's single war-hardened legion and experienced auxiliaries could have indeed subjugated all of Ireland in a few short campaigns.

In the final work of his life, the *Annals*, Tacitus also briefly mentions Ireland in the context of Roman military movements in Britain three decades before Agricola's governorship:

> *iamque ventum haud procul mari, quod Hiberniam insulam aspectat.* (*Annals* 12.32)

> And now [Ostorius] came near to the sea, which looks toward *Hibernia*.

Publius Ostorius took over as governor of Britain in A.D. 47, and in the following year he launched a campaign against the Deceangli tribe of northern Wales. He had expanded Roman control almost to the Irish Sea when a revolt by the Brigantes forced him to abandon his westward advance mentioned here.

Juvenal

Very little is known about the life of the Roman satirist Juvenal aside from the fact that he composed his biting social criticisms during the early part of the second century A.D. His satires cover all the perceived ills of Roman society but focus primarily on the corruption of the wealthy urban elite. His one brief reference to Ireland is found in *Satire* 2, where he denounces the shallow morality and sexual debauchery of supposed moral philosophers. After cataloguing the hypocritical behavior of these would-be Stoics, he ends by contrasting recent Roman military victories with the deplorable state of morals in Rome itself:

> *arma quidem ultra*
> *litora Iuvernae promovimus et modo captas*
> *Orcadas ac minima contentos nocte Britannos;*
> *sed quae nunc populi fiunt victoris in urbe,*
> *non faciunt illi quos vicimus.* (*Satire* 2.159–63)

> Indeed, we have advanced arms beyond the shores
> of *Iuverna* and the recently captured Orkneys
> and the mighty Britons with their short nights;

but the deeds we perform in our victorious city
will never be done by the men we have conquered.

For several reasons, we should be wary of taking this passage literally as evidence that the Romans, even for a short time, invaded Ireland.[103] First, satire is a genre of deliberate exaggeration, and Juvenal and his satirical predecessors (such as Lucilius and Horace) frequently overstated a situation for poetic and rhetorical effect. This satire in fact uses geographical hyperbole at its beginning, when Juvenal despairs that he would rather flee to the ends of the earth among the Sarmatians and the frozen sea than live among hypocritical moralists; matching hyperbole at the end of the poem therefore would not be out of place.[104] The phrase *ultra litora Iuvernae* is probably an example of such hyperbole (though to be fair to those who would argue otherwise, *ultra litora* does clearly and simply mean "inland from the shore" in its only other occurrence in Latin).[105] Second, there is no clear archaeological evidence for the presence of a Roman army in Ireland. Third, if the Romans had conquered Ireland or any part of Ireland, why is Tacitus conspicuously silent on the subject? He specifically notes that Agricola wanted to invade Ireland and made hopeful preparations to do so, but he does not say that Roman soldiers ever landed on the island.

On the other hand, the above arguments may not be convincing to critics who support the idea of a Roman invasion. First, they might say, if Juvenal is only using exaggerated rhetoric when he claims that Roman armies have pushed beyond Ireland's shore, it is strange that he pairs this hyperbole with the campaigns in the Orkneys and Britain, both historically attested actions.[106] Second, a Roman army would not necessarily leave behind clear archaeological remains, especially if the invasion were short-lived. An archaeologist would be equally hard-pressed to identify unambiguous remains of Caesar's large but temporary expeditions into Britain in 55–54 B.C. Finally, would a short military incursion into Ireland necessarily have been recorded by Tacitus, who rapidly moves through Agricola's campaigns from Wales to northern Scotland in a series of very short chapters? Perhaps Tacitus felt a minor and possibly unsuccessful campaign against Ireland simply was not important to his readers and his purpose.

In the final analysis, it is possible that Juvenal refers to an actual expedition into Ireland by a Roman force, but, given the genre in which he writes and the lack of supporting evidence, a prudent reader should be hesitant to take this passage as proof of a Roman military invasion of Ireland.

Dionysius Periegetes

Almost nothing is known of Dionysius Periegetes ("The Guide"), who probably wrote his geographical survey of the inhabitable world sometime in the early second century A.D. His hexameter poem of just over 1,180 lines describes the known world from Ethiopia to Scythia to northern Europe, including a brief reference to the two *Bretanides* islands, though he does not specifically name Britain or Ireland:

> ἄλλαι δ' Ὠκεανοῖο παραὶ βορεώτιδας ἀκτὰς
> δισσαὶ νῆσοι ἔασι Βρετανίδες, ἀντία Ῥήνου·
> κεῖθι γὰρ ὑστατίην ἀπερεύγεται εἰς ἅλα δίνην.
> Τάων τοι μέγεθος περιώσιον, οὐδέ τις ἄλλη
> νήσοις ἐν πάσῃσι Βρετανίσιν ἰσοφαρίζει.
> (*Orbis descriptio* 565–69 [*Geographi Graeci Minores* 2.140])

Two other islands, the *Bretanides*, are near the northern shore of
  the Ocean, opposite the Rhine,
from there it sends forth its final eddies into the sea. Great is their
  size, nor do any other
islands equal the *Bretanides*.

Dionysius does not claim originality in his survey and is clearly drawing on earlier Greek geographers. In describing the *Bretanides* islands as the largest known, he is in the same tradition as the earlier Pseudo-Aristotle.[107]

Ptolemy

Ptolemy (Claudius Ptolemaeus) was one of the most important writers on mathematics, astronomy, and geography in the ancient world; his influence has been felt even into modern times. He also far exceeds any ancient author before or after him in his detailed and generally accurate description of the geography of Ireland.

Almagest

Ptolemy first mentions Ireland as "Little Britain" (Μικρὰ Βρεττανία) while discussing latitudes in his earliest astronomical work, known through later Arabic translations as the *Almagest:* [108]

εἰκοστὸς πέμπτος ἐστὶ παράλληλος καθ᾽ ὃν ἂν γένοιτο ἡ μεγίστη ἡμέρα
ὡρῶν ἰσημερινῶν ιη΄. Ἀπέχει δ᾽οὗτος τοῦ ἰσημερινοῦ μοιρῶν νη΄· καὶ γράφεται διὰ τῶν νοτίων τῆς μικρᾶς Βρεττανίας.

εἰκοστὸς ἕκτος ἐστὶ παράλληλος καθ᾽ ὃν ἂν γένοιτο ἡ μεγίστη ἡμέρα ὡρῶν
ἰσημερινῶν ιη΄ ς΄΄. Ἀπέχει δ᾽οὗτος τοῦ ἰσημερινοῦ μοιρῶν νθ΄ ς΄΄· καὶ γράφεται διὰ τῶν μέσων τῆς μικρᾶς Βρεττανίας.

καὶ ὅπου μὲν τοίνυν ἡ μεγίστη ἡμέρα ὡρῶν ἐστιν ἰσημερινῶν ιθ΄, ἐκεῖνος
ὁ παράλληλος ἀπέχει τοῦ ἰσημερινοῦ μοιρῶν ξα΄. καὶ γράφεται διὰ τῶν
βορείων τῆς μικρᾶς Βρεττανίας. (*Almagest* 2.6.25–27 [Heiberg 1898])

The twenty-fifth parallel has a longest day of 18 equatorial hours.
This is 58 degrees from the equator and passes through the southern
part of *Mikra Brettania*.

The twenty-sixth parallel has a longest day of 18.5 equatorial hours.
This is 59.5 degrees from the equator and passes through the middle
of *Mikra Brettania*.

The parallel where the longest day is 19 equatorial hours is 61 degrees
from the equator and passes through the northern parts of *Mikra
Brettania*.

Ptolemy begins his survey of latitudes at the equator and continues
north through Ireland to the pole. He is the only ancient writer to use the
name "Little Britain" for Ireland, though in doing so he is well within the
tradition of earlier authors who pair a smaller Ireland with a larger Britain
as the two Brettanic Isles.[109] Ptolemy's placement of Ireland at a latitude between 58 and 61 degrees errs too far to the north, but is considerably more
accurate than Strabo's, which places Ireland several degrees closer to the
pole.[110] Ireland actually extends from a latitude of just south of 52 degrees
to just north of 55 degrees. Ptolemy maintains this placement of Ireland
in his *Geography*, with the southernmost point in Ireland at 57 degrees and
the northernmost points at 61 degrees 30 minutes.

Geography

Like most ancient geographers, Ptolemy does not claim to base his work
on first-hand observations. The Introduction of his *Geography* instead reveals that his study is a compilation of earlier geographical writings sub-

jected to careful scrutiny and reasoned analysis, favoring the accounts of established geographers over those of travelers. The source on which he especially relies is the geographer Marinus of Tyre, to the point that the *Geography* in many ways seems an expansion and correction of the previous work of Marinus. Unfortunately, the original work of Marinus does not survive, and we know nothing of this writer aside from the comments of Ptolemy in his Introduction. We do not even know exactly when Marinus lived, though he cannot have written long before the composition of the *Geography*, as Ptolemy calls him the latest of the geographers "of our time." [111] Ptolemy clearly has the greatest respect for Marinus' work, yet he feels the need to correct many of his predecessor's errors. As related by Ptolemy, Marinus carefully surveyed the writings of earlier geographers and historians, and drew as well upon the first-hand accounts of many travelers. These accounts include voyages of Greek sailors to India, Roman expeditions to Africa, voyages to the Canary Islands, and Macedonian merchant expeditions to central Asia and China.[112] Marinus does complain that merchants are generally not the most reliable sources for geographic information, because their primary concern is understandably commerce, not scientific exploration, and because they exaggerate distances due to a love of boasting. As an example, Ptolemy relates the objections of Marinus to the account of Philemon, derived from merchants, concerning the width of Ireland:

ἔοικε δὲ καὶ αὐτὸς ἀπιστεῖν ταῖς τῶν ἐμπορευομένων ἱστορίαις· τῷ γοῦν τοῦ Φιλήμονος λόγῳ, δι᾽ οὗ τὸ μῆκος τῆς Ἰουερνίας νήσου τὸ ἀπ᾽ ἀνατολῶν ἐπὶ δυσμὰς ἡμερῶν εἴκοσι παραδέδωκεν, οὐ συγκατατίθεται διὰ τὸ φάναι αὐτὸν (ὑπὸ) ἐμπόρων ἀκηκοέναι. (*Geography* 1.11)

Marinus seems to disbelieve the reports of merchants, at least the statement of Philemon that the length of the island *Iwernia* is twenty days from east to west, because Philemon said that he had heard it from traders.

As with Marinus, we know almost nothing of Philemon aside from these brief remarks of Ptolemy, only that he is probably the same source used by Pliny on the North Sea and Baltic areas.[113] But the passage does give us an important hint at Ptolemy's sources of information on Ireland—that along with the writings of earlier geographers, he included information ultimately derived from merchants visiting the island, regardless of the distaste and mistrust of merchants expressed by Marinus and himself.

This passage also confirms the earlier statement of Tacitus that merchants were visiting Ireland and is again supported by the archaeological evidence of Roman finds throughout the island.[114] The statement, derived from merchants who had visited Ireland, that it is a journey of twenty days from east to west across the island is not really as preposterous as Marinus seemed to have believed. Depending on where one begins and ends, Ireland is roughly 250 kilometers from east to west, which breaks down to approximately 12.5 kilometers per day over twenty days. Slow travel, perhaps, but given Ireland's landscape of hills and bogs, along with the need of merchants for frequent stops to conduct business, it is believable. Regardless of whether we accept the exact figure given by these merchants, the more important inference to draw from this passage is that traders were not just visiting the shores of the island, as reported by Tacitus, but were also venturing into the interior of Ireland. This helps to explain the ultimate sources for Ptolemy's extensive list of inland Irish tribes and towns. As always, we should not go too far and assume that Roman merchants were constantly crisscrossing Ireland and staging traveling bazaars at every hill fort and village in the land, but the passage does provide a suggestive glimpse of at least occasional travel by foreign traders into interior Ireland during Roman times.

Ptolemy calls Ireland "Little Britain" in the *Almagest*, but here in the *Geography* he is the first to use a new name for Ireland, *Iwernia* ('Ιουερνία). The introduction of -*w*- into a Greek name for Ireland is further evidence for increasing direct contact with Irish natives, who used the *w*-sound in their native name *Iweriu. Even though the Greeks of his era did not normally use the *w*-sound in their language, Ptolemy was often careful to preserve names close to their native forms.

Book Two of Ptolemy's *Geography* begins with a prologue that describes western Europe and includes his first map, which covers Ireland and Britain:

ΒΙΒΛΙΟΝ ΔΕΥΤΕΡΟΝ	Second Book
τάδε ἔνεστιν ἐν τῷ δευτέρῳ βιβλίῳ	The following is in the second book:
πρόλογος τῆς κατὰ μέρος ὑφηγήσεως.	A prologue of the particular descriptions

ἔκθεσις τοῦ δυσμικωτέρου τῆς	A description of the western parts
Εὐρώπης μέρους κατὰ τὰς	of Europe according to the
ὑποκειμένας ἐπαρχίας ἢ σατραπείας.	provinces or prefectures it
	includes
αʹ. Ἰουερνίας νήσου Πρεττανικῆς.	1. The Prettanic Isle *Iwernia*
Πίναξ αʹ.	(Map 1)
βʹ. Ἀλουίωνος νήσου Πρεττανικῆς	2. The Prettanic Isle *Albion*

Ptolemy continues the pairing of Britain and Ireland as in his *Almagest*, though in this instance, the older term *Prettania* (Πρεττανικῆς) is found in most manuscripts rather than the *Brettania* (Βρεττανίας) of the *Almagest*.[115]

In this prologue, Ptolemy also explains that, while his coordinates of latitude and longitude are admittedly incomplete and uncertain in some instances, his *Geography* is designed as an aid in the creation of accurate maps. He even welcomes corrections and additions from future research. He also notes that his work is primarily one of geography, not ethnography, so that the particular features of religion, customs, and commerce for the tribes he will list are not generally noted.[116]

After the prologue, Ptolemy begins his description of the world, starting with Ireland as the most distant part of western Europe. In this section, as with islands elsewhere in his *Geography*, the description generally follows a periplus style of exploring first the coasts, then inland areas and nearby islands in a systematic manner. Ptolemy lists by latitude and longitude conspicuous coastal features such as promontories, river mouths, and towns near the shoreline or inland. He also notes both coastal and inland tribal names, though he does not give specific coordinates for these, only relative locations. Ptolemy calls a town in his list a *polis* (πόλις), but students of Greek history should not think of the cities such as Athens or Sparta normally associated with this term. Rather, a *polis* in Ptolemy seems to be any settled location worthy of a name, whether a bustling city such as Roman London or a backwater settlement in Italy, Ethiopia, Scythia, or Ireland.

On the whole, Ptolemy's portrayal of Ireland is reasonably accurate given the island's distant location on the edge of the known world (see Fig. 18). The generally southwestern bulge of Kerry and the northeastern protrusion of Ulster are both shown, as is the southeastern cape near Wexford. The western extension of Connemara is poorly indicated, but this would likely be the area least visited by merchants from Gaul or Brit-

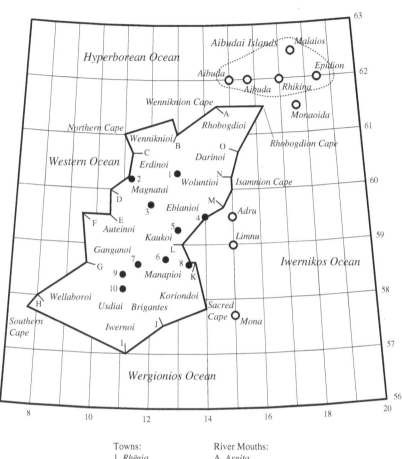

Towns:
1. *Rhēgia*
2. *Magnata*
3. *Rhaiba*
4. *Eblana*
5. *Labēros*
6. *Dunon*
7. *Makolikon*
8. *Manapia*
9. *Rhēgia (other)*
10. *Iwernis*

River Mouths:
A. *Argita*
B. *Widua*
C. *Rhawiu*
D. *Libniu*
E. *Ausoba*
F. *Sēnu*
G. *Dur*
H. *Iernu*
I. *Dabrōna*
J. *Birgu*
K. *Modonnu*
L. *Oboka*
M. *Buwinda*
N. *Winderios*
O. *Logia*

FIGURE 18. Ptolemy's Map of Ireland

ain. The eastern shore, however, is less accurately drawn than we might expect for the coast presumably most visited by Roman merchants. The length of Ireland in Ptolemy is tolerably close to modern measurements, and Ptolemy (or Marinus) also places Ireland much closer to Britain than to Spain, correcting an almost constant mistake in earlier writers.[117]

An established and reasonable approach to Ptolemy's description of Ireland has been to compare the text of the *Geography* to medieval or modern maps, then see which features of Ptolemy best match the headlands, rivers, tribes, and towns of later Ireland.[118] These efforts have yielded many persuasive results, yet some attempts have also produced highly speculative correspondence between Ptolemy and Irish features, tribes, and towns known from later literature or archaeology. Thus the best approach seems to be to make a conservative analysis of Ptolemy's geographical description of Ireland with many necessary qualifications of "perhaps" and "possibly" rather than to compile a deceptively certain list of matching pairs. The same caution is warranted for etymological speculation on the meaning and origin of Irish names listed by Ptolemy. In some cases, a reasonably certain etymology can be put forward, but in many others the clear meaning of a name is simply unknown. This is especially true when we consider the permutations the Irish names may have undergone on their journey from the shores of Ireland to Ptolemy's writing desk in Egypt. The merchants who were presumably the first link in the chain were probably Celtic-speaking Britons and Gauls with a language similar to Irish, but different enough that they would have made certain linguistic changes in reported Irish words. For example, the Britons and Gauls, as well as the Greeks of this era, did not have a *q* [k^w] sound in their language, as did the Irish and Romans, so that any *q* in an Irish name would probably have been changed to a similar sound, such as *p*, by a British or Gaulish merchant. Thus an Irish word beginning, for example, with *maq-* would likely end up as *map-* before it reached Ptolemy. An English speaker might perform a similar alteration in transcribing the German city of *München* as a more pronounceable *Munich*, the Indian river *Ganga* as *Ganges*, or the *Aaraxpeahu* tribe of the western United States as *Arapaho*. Add to such linguistically driven permutations the inevitable deformations of a word or phrase as it is passed down the line of sources and we can see why a cautious approach to the etymology of Ptolemy's Irish names is necessary.

The North Coast

ΚΕΦ. Β΄.			Chapter Two		
Ἰουερνίας νήσου Πρεττανικῆς θέσις. (Εὐρώπης πίναξ α΄)[119]			Position of the Prettanic Isle *Iwernia* (Europe, Map 1)		
ἀρκτικῆς πλευρᾶς περιγραφή, ἧς ὑπέρκειται. Ὠκεανὸς Ὑπερβόρειος.			A description of the northern coast, beyond which lies the Hyperborean Ocean		
Βόρειον ἄκρον	ια΄	ξα΄	Northern Cape	11°	61°
Οὐεννίκνιον ἄκρον	ιβ΄ ν΄	ξα΄ κ΄	*Wenniknion* Cape	12° 50′	61° 20′
Οὐιδούα ποταμοῦ ἐκβολαί	ιγ΄	ξα΄	Mouth of the *Widua* River	13°	61°
Ἀργίτα ποταμοῦ ἐκβολαί	ιδ΄ ʟ″	ξα΄ ʟ″	Mouth of the *Argita* River	14° 30′	61° 30′
Ῥοβόγδιον ἄκρον	ιϛ΄ γ″	ξα΄ ʟ″	*Rhobogdion* Cape	16° 20′	61° 30′
παροικοῦσι δὲ τὴν πλευρὰν ἀπὸ μὲν δυσμῶν Οὐεννίκνιοι· εἶτα ἐφεξῆς καὶ πρὸς ἀνατολὰς Ῥοβόγδιοι.			The *Wenniknioi* inhabit the western coast; next to them on the east are the *Rhobogdioi*		

Most of the names above, as throughout Ptolemy's description of Ireland, cannot be absolutely identified or matched with names from later records, though some reasonable guesses can be made based largely on position, and to a lesser extent on subsequent place names (see Fig. 19). A few of the names are Greek terms assigned by Ptolemy or earlier authors, but most appear to be native Irish names derived ultimately from merchants and visitors. The term *Hyberborean* (Ὑπερβόρειος) for the Atlantic Ocean north of Ireland is almost unique to Ptolemy and is based on the Greek adjective *hyperboreos* (ὑπερβόρεος), meaning literally "beyond the North Wind," or more commonly, "extreme north."[120] Likewise, the cape called *Boreion* is simply from the Greek adjective *boreios* (βόρειος, "northern"), which Ptolemy also uses for a northern promontory in distant Taprobane.[121] This *Boreion* Cape, which may be Bloody Foreland Head in County Donegal or possibly Rossan Point, is not the northernmost prom-

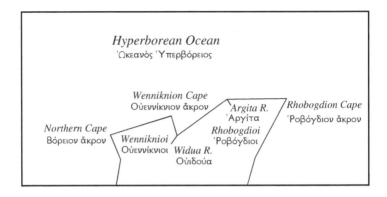

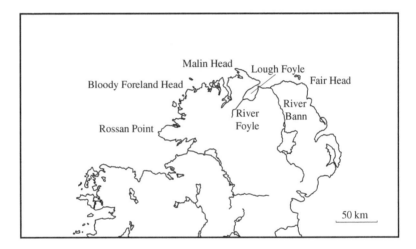

FIGURE 19. The North Coast

ontory on Ptolemy's map of Ireland, in spite of its name. *Wenniknion* Cape (*Οὐεννίκνιον ἄκρον*) matches Malin Head reasonably well and shares its name with the nearby *Wenniknioi* tribe. The large central depression on Ptolemy's map of the north coast fits very nicely with Lough Foyle at the mouth of the River Foyle near modern Derry, making this river a likely candidate for Ptolemy's *Widua* River. If the *Widua* is the Foyle, then the *Argita* (*Ἀργίτα*) should be the River Bann just to the east. *Rhobogdion* Cape (*Ῥοβόγδιον ἄκρον*) and the *Rhobogdioi* tribe should be in the area of Fair Head at the beginning of the southeastern turn of the Irish coast.

The West Coast

δυτικῆς πλευρᾶς περιγραφή, ᾗ παράκειται Δυτικὸς Ὠκεανός.			A description of the western coast, bordering on the Western Ocean		
μετὰ τὸ Βόρειον ἄκρον, ὅ ἐστιν	ια'	ξα'	After the Northern Cape, which is	11°	61°
Ῥαουίου ποταμοῦ ἐκβολαί	ια' γ"	ξ' γο"	Mouth of the *Rhawiu* River	11° 20'	60° 40'
Μάγγατα πόλις [ἐπίσημος]	ια' δ"	ξ' δ"	City of *Magnata* [designated]	11° 15'	60° 15'
Λιβνίου ποταμοῦ ἐκβολαί	ι' ʟ"	ξ'	Mouth of the *Libniu* River	10° 30'	60°
Αὐσόβα ποταμοῦ ἐκβολαί	ι' ʟ"	νθ' ʟ"	Mouth of the *Ausoba* River	10° 30'	59° 30'
Σήνου ποταμοῦ ἐκβολαί	θ' ʟ"	νθ' ʟ"	Mouth of the *Sēnu* River	9° 30'	59° 30'
Δούρ ποταμοῦ ἐκβολαί	θ' γο"	νη' γο"	Mouth of the *Dur* River	9° 40'	58° 40'
Ἰέρνου ποταμοῦ ἐκβολαί	η'	νη'	Mouth of the *Iernu* River	8°	58°
Νότιον ἄκρον	ζ' γο"	νζ' ʟ"δ"	Southern Cape	7° 40'	57° 45'
παροικοῦσι δὲ τὴν πλευρὰν μετὰ τοὺς Οὐεννικνίους Ἐρδῖνοι, ὑφ' οὓς Μαγνᾶται· εἶτα Αὐτεῖνοι· εἶτα Γαγγανοὶ, ὑφ' οὓς Οὐελλάβοροι.			The *Erdinoi* inhabit this coast after the *Wenniknioi*, below these the *Magnatai*, then the *Auteinoi*, then the *Ganganoi*, and below them the *Wellaboroi*		

The western coast is the most poorly represented area of Ireland in Ptolemy compared to the modern map, so that identifications are here the most speculative (see Fig. 20). The *Dutikos* Ocean (Δυτικὸς Ὠκεανός) again simply uses a Greek adjective, *dutikos* (δυτικός), meaning "western," for the Atlantic Ocean west of Ireland. The *Rhawiu* (Ῥαουίου) River fits well with the River Erne flowing into the major indentation of Donegal Bay.[122]

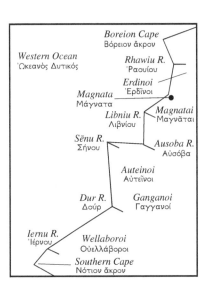

FIGURE 20. The West Coast

South of the *Rhawiu* River is the only settlement listed on the west coast of Ireland, *Magnata* (Μάγγατα πόλις), the polis of the *Magnatai* (Μαγνᾶται) tribe, which may have been located in County Mayo.[123] The mouth of the *Libniu* (Λιβνίου) River may be Clew Bay, while the *Ausoba* (Αὐσόβα) river mouth could be Galway Bay. The *Sēnu* (Σήνου) River has often been taken as the Shannon, and there seems little reason to disagree, as its positions on the ancient and modern maps correspond reasonably well, though the *Sēnu* is a little farther north than the Shannon's location. Ptolemy's name is also a tolerably close match to the Old Irish name for the river, *Sinann* or *Sinna*, which may have been **Senuna* in the second century A.D. The mouths of the *Dur* (Δούρ) and *Iernu* (Ἰέρνου) rivers may be Dingle Bay and the mouth of the Kenmare River, respectively. The river named *Iernu* may have lost a *w* in transmission and may originally have been **Iwernu*, more closely matching the nearby *Iwernoi* (Ἰουέρνοι) tribe and *Iwernis* (Ἰουερνίς) town, all based

74

on the *Iwerion- root underlying the original name of Ireland itself.[124] The physical features of Ptolemy's western coast end at the *Notion* promontory (Νότιον ἄκρον), again a Greek term, *notios* (νότιος), meaning "southern." It is difficult to say which of the capes in County Kerry or County Cork is intended by this designation, but Slea Head, Bray Head, Dursey Head, and Mizen Head are all likely candidates. The long stretch of the western coast contains five tribes, beginning with the *Erdinoi* ('Ερδῖνοι) in the area of Donegal Bay. The *Magnatai* (Μαγνᾶται) tribe presumably inhabited the regions of County Mayo around the polis of *Magnata* (Μάγνατα). The *Auteinoi* (Αὐτεῖνοι) might be placed somewhere near the Shannon River or to the north in County Galway, while the *Ganganoi* (Γαγγανοί) are to their south. The final tribe of the west is the *Wellaboroi* (Οὐελλάβοροι) in the far southwest, whom the fifth-century writer Orosius calls the *Velabri*.[125]

The South Coast

τῆς ἐφεξῆς μεσημβρινῆς πλευρᾶς περιγραφή, ᾗ παράκειται Ὠκεανὸς Οὐεργιόνιος.			A successive description of the southern coast, which borders the *Wergionios* Ocean		
μετὰ τὸ Νότιον ἄκρον, ὅ ἐστιν	ζ′ γο″	νζ′ L″δ″	After the Southern Cape, which is	7° 40′	57° 45′
Δαβρώνα ποταμοῦ ἐκβολαί	ια′ δ″	νζ′	Mouth of the *Dabrōna* River	11° 15′	57°
Βίργου ποταμοῦ ἐκβολαί	ιβ′ L″	νζ′ L″	Mouth of the *Birgu* River	12° 30′	57° 30′
Ἱερὸν ἄκρον.	ιδ′	νζ′ L″γ″	Sacred Cape	14°	57° 50′
παροικοῦσι δὲ τὴν πλευρὰν μετὰ τοὺς Οὐελλαβόρους Ἰούερνοι, ὑπὲρ οὓς Οὐσδίαι καὶ ἀνατολικώτεροι. Βρίγαντες.			The *Iwernoi* inhabit the coast after the *Wellaboroi*, above these are the *Usdiai*, and farther to the east are the *Brigantes*		

Ptolemy's southern coast begins at whichever of the promontories of Counties Kerry or Cork he intends as the Southern Cape and extends first southeast to the mouth of the *Dabrōna* River, then northeast to the Sacred

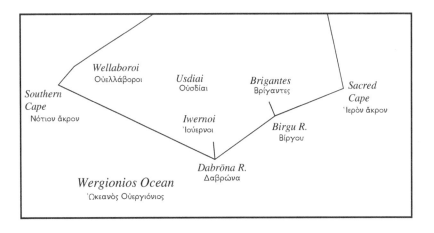

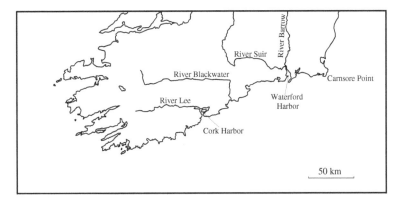

FIGURE 21. The South Coast

Cape (see Fig. 21). In reality, Ireland's south coast rises ever gradually to the northeast along its entire length. The *Wergionios* Ocean ('Ωκεανὸς Οὐεργιόνιος), named only by Ptolemy and Marcianus, lies to the south of Ireland.[126] The *Dabrōna* (Δαβρώνα) River is well placed on Ptolemy's map to be the River Lee flowing into the prominent recess of Cork Harbor. The older Irish name of this river was the *Sabrann*, perhaps from an even older *Sabrona*, suggesting that somewhere along the chain of geographical or textual transmission, a D- may have replaced an original S-.[127] The mouth of the *Birgu* (Βίργου) River should be Waterford Harbor, into which flows the River Barrow.[128] The southern coast ends at the Sacred Cape ('Ιερὸν ἄκρον), which can be no other than Carnsore Point. The use of the term "sacred" is reminiscent of Avienus' name for Ireland, but a connection is not necessarily warranted, as there were other sacred capes in the classical world, as in the Iberian peninsula.[129] The tribes of the southern coast include the *Iwernoi* (Ἰούερνοι), discussed previously, and the *Usdiai* (Οὐσδίαι) above them. In the southeast dwelled the *Brigantes* (Βρίγαντες), a tribe often seen as emigrants or refugees from the better-known Brigantes of northern England. While this is possible, it is worth remembering that many places and groups throughout the ancient Celtic world bore similar names.[130]

The East Coast

ἀνατολικῆς πλευρᾶς περιγραφὴ, ᾗ παράκειται Ὠκεανὸς καλούμενος Ἰουερνικός.			A description of the east coast, which borders on the ocean called *Iwernikos*		
μετὰ τὸ Ἱερὸν ἄκρον, ὅ ἐστι	ιδ′	νζ′ L″γ″	After the Sacred Cape, which is	14°	57° 50′
Μοδόννου ποταμοῦ ἐκβολαί	ιγ′ γο″	νη′ γο″	Mouth of the *Modonnu* River	13° 40′	58° 40′
Μαναπία πόλις	ιγ′ L″	νη′ γο″	City of *Manapia*	13° 30′	58° 40′
Ὀβόκα ποταμοῦ ἐκβολαί	ιγ′ s″	νθ′	Mouth of the *Oboka* River	13° 10′	59°
Ἔβλανα πόλις	ιδ′	νθ′ L″	City of *Eblana*	14°	59° 30′
Βουουίνδα ποταμοῦ ἐκβολαί	ιδ′ γο″	νθ′ γο″	Mouth of the *Buwinda* River	14° 40′	59° 40′
Ἰσάμνιον [ἄκρον]	ιε′	ξ′	*Isamnion* [Cape]	15°	60°
Οὐινδέριος ποταμοῦ ἐκβολαί	ιε′	ξ′ δ″	Mouth of the *Winderios* River	15°	60° 15′
Λογία ποταμοῦ ἐκβολαί	ιε′ γ″	ξ′ γο″	Mouth of the *Logia* River	15° 20′	60° 40′

μεθ' ἃς τὸ Ῥοβόγδιον ἄκρον

παροικοῦσι δὲ καὶ ταύτην τὴν
πλευρὰν μετὰ τοὺς Ῥοβογδίους
Δαρῖνοι, ὑφ' οὓς Οὐολούντιοι· εἶτα
Ἐβλάνιοι· εἶτα Καῦκοι, ὑφ' οὓς
Μανάπιοι· εἶτα Κοριονδοὶ ὑπὲρ τοὺς
Βρίγαντας.

After which is the *Rhobogdion* Cape

The *Darinoi* inhabit this side after
the *Rhobogdioi*, after which the
Woluntioi, then the *Eblanioi*, then the
Kaukoi, below them the *Manapioi*;
Brigantes
then the *Koriondoi* live above the

Since the eastern coast of Ireland faced Roman Britain, and since more Roman artifacts have been unearthed there than anywhere else on the island, we might reasonably expect this shore to be the most fully and accurately represented area of Ptolemy's Ireland. Indeed, Ptolemy does list six tribes, five river mouths, and two coastal towns on the east coast—more features than are given for the other shores, aside from the six river mouths of the highly indented western side of Ireland. But it is surprisingly difficult to match modern features on this shore to the ancient map (see Fig. 22). For example, the mouth of the *Modonnu* (Μοδόννου) River, the first feature on the eastern shore, should reasonably be the end of the River Slaney at Wexford Harbor, a feature too prominent to omit purposely, except that the *Modonnu* is much too far north on the ancient map and has no sharp westward turn just to its north, as Ptolemy represents it. This westward turn at the southern end of a large bay more closely resembles the area from Killiney Bay into Dublin Bay, but there is no river near Killiney Bay to match the *Modonnu*. If Wexford Harbor has been omitted in the ancient text, the *Modonnu* might be the river called the Avoca on modern maps, though this name probably derives from Ptolemy's *Oboka* (Ὀβόκα) farther north. The polis of *Manapia* (Μαναπία), immediately to the west of the *Modonnu* river mouth, is a town of the *Manapioi* (Μανάπιοι) tribe. The names of both the town and the people call to mind not only the *Menapii* tribe of Gaul, but also Pliny's nearby island of *Monapia*, which may be the Isle of Man.[131] The names contain a very un-Irish *p*, but if these inhabitants of eastern Ireland had recently migrated from Gaul, where *p* was used, it would not be surprising to find it here. On the other hand, this could easily be a case of British merchants, who also used *p* but not *q* in their language, distorting an Irish word originally pronounced something like *Manaqioi*. In the bay just to the northwest of *Manapia* is the *Oboka* (Ὀβόκα) River, matching well the position but not the name of the modern Liffey flowing through Dublin town. The town of *Eblana* (Ἔβλανα) and its matching

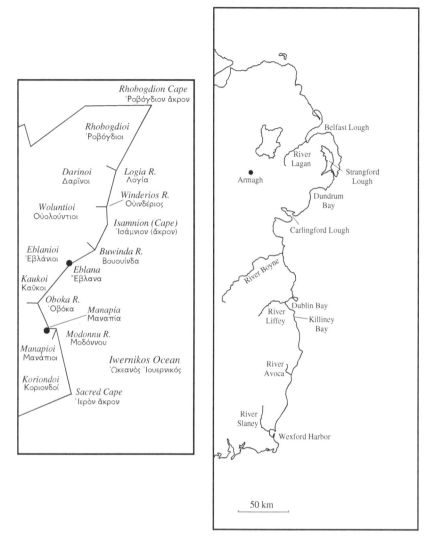

FIGURE 22. The East Coast

tribe the *Eblanioi* ('Εβλάνιοι) were probably located in northern County Dublin, though there is no connection between the name of the Viking-era town of Dublin (*Dub-linn*, "black pool") and ancient *Eblana*. The *Buwinda* (Βουουίνδα) River is almost certainly the Boyne (Old Irish *Boend*) of County Meath, along which many Roman artifacts have been unearthed.[132]

79

Some manuscripts list *Isamnion* (᾽Ισάμνιον) as a promontory (ἄκρον), but it is possible that it was instead a town to the north of the Buwinda.[133] The mouths of the *Winderios* (Οὐινδέριος) and *Logia* (Λογία) rivers are the remaining physical features of the eastern coast, which may be, respectively, Carlingford Lough, Dundrum Bay, or Strangford Lough and the Lagan River, which flows into Belfast Lough (*Loch Loíg*).[134] The six tribes of the east coast begin with the *Koriondoi* (Κοριονδοί) in the south above the *Brigantes*, followed by the *Manapioi* discussed above. The *Kaukoi* (Καῦκοι) may have lived in the area around modern Dublin and are not likely to be related to the *Cauci* of Germany, in spite of the similarity in names.[135] After the *Eblanioi* were the *Woluntioi* (Οὐολούντιοι), probably the ancestors of the *Ulaid* tribe, celebrated in medieval Irish tales such as the *Táin Bó Cúailnge*, with their chief town being Emain Macha near Armagh. Finally, the *Darinoi* (Δαρῖνοι) inhabited the far northeastern coast below the *Rhobogdioi*.

The Inland Cities

πόλεις δέ εἰσι μεσόγειοι αἵδε·			These are the inland cities:		
῾Ρηγία	ιγ′	ξ′ γ″	Rhēgia	13°	60° 20′
῾Ραῖβα	ιβ′	νθ′ ∟″δ″	Rhaiba	12°	59° 45′
Λάβηρος	ιγ′	νθ′ δ″	Labēros	13°	59° 15′
Μακόλικον	ια′ ∟″	νη′ γο″	Makolikon	11° 30′	58° 40′
῾Ρηγία ἑτέρα	ια′	νθ′ ∟″	Another *Rhēgia*	11°	58° 30′
Δοῦνον	ιβ′ ∟″	νη′ ∟″δ″	Dunon	12° 30′	58° 45′
᾽Ιουερνίς	ια′	νη′ ϛ″	Iwernis	11°	58° 10′

Although none of the settlements can be identified with any certainty, a few comments are necessary. *Rhēgia* (῾Ρηγία) could be a Greek ap-

proximate of a native Celtic term *rigia ("royal seat"), but it is more likely
to be a Latin word of the same meaning (regia). The northern and southern towns by this name were apparently both seats of tribal kings. The
southeastern city of Dunon (Δοῦνον) bears the common Celtic name for
a fort or hill fort (Gaulish dunon, Old Irish dún, Welsh din). Town names
using this same term are found in Britain and Gaul, and throughout the
Celtic world.[136]

The Islands

ὑπέρκεινται δὲ νῆσοι τῆς Ἰουερνίας αἵ τε καλούμεναι Αἰβοῦδαι πέντε τὸν ἀριθμὸν, ὧν ἡ μὲν δυτικωτέρα καλεῖται			Above *Iwernia* lie islands that are called the *Aibudai*, five in number, of which the most westerly is called		
Αἰβοῦδα	ιε′	ξβ′	Aibuda	15°	62°
ἡ δ' ἐφεξῆς αὐτῆς πρὸς ἀνατολὰς			After this to the east:		
ὁμοίως Αἰβοῦδα	ιε′ γο′	ξβ′	Another *Aibuda*	15°	62° 40′
εἶτα Ῥικίνα	ιζ′	ξβ′	Then *Rhikina*	17°	62°
εἶτα Μαλαῖος	ιζ′ ʟ″	ξβ′ ʟ″	Then *Malaios*	17° 30′	62° 30′
εἶτα Ἐπίδιον	ιη′ ʟ″	ξβ′	Then *Epidion*	18° 30′	62°
καὶ ἀπ' ἀνατολῶν τῆς Ἰουερνίας εἰσὶν αἵδε νῆσοι·			To the east of *Iwernia* are these islands:		
Μονάοιδα	ιζ′ γο″	ξα′ ʟ″	*Monaoida*	17° 40′	61° 30′
Μόνα νῆσος	ιε′	νζ′ γο″	*Mona* Island	15°	57° 40′

῎Αδρου ἔρημος	ιε′	νθ′ ∟″	*Adru*, desolate	15°	59° 30′
Λίμνου ἔρημος	ιε′	νθ′	*Limnu*, desolate	15°	59°

The islands listed by Ptolemy to the north and east of Ireland are unique in that a number of them are also noted in various forms by earlier authors, providing a basis of comparison generally unavailable elsewhere in his description of Ireland (see Fig. 23). Several if not most of the islands associated here with Ireland are actually closer and more historically tied to Britain. The five *Aibudai* (Αἰβοῦδαι) are elsewhere called the *Ebudai* by Ptolemy, though they are not there numbered; they are first noted by Pliny, however, as the thirty *Hebudes*.[137] These are almost certainly the Hebrides, closer to the northwest coast of Scotland than to Ireland. Two namesake islands, both called *Aibuda* (Αἰβοῦδα), define the western boundary of this group, while just to their east *Rhikina* (Ῥικίνα), Pliny's *Riginia*, may be Rathlin Island off County Antrim.[138] *Malaios* (Μαλαῖος) is the northernmost of this group and may be the Isle of Mull.[139] The eastern island of *Epidion* (᾽Επίδιον) is the final member of Ptolemy's *Aibudai* group. It is almost certainly related to the Scottish tribe of *Epidioi* (᾽Επίδιοι) occupying the *Epidion* (᾽Επίδιον) promontory, modern Kintyre.[140] The peninsula of Kintyre is so thinly attached to the mainland that it could easily be mistaken for an island and here may be a duplication on Ptolemy's part. *Monaoida* (Μονάοιδα), just to the south of the *Aibudai*, is probably the Isle of Man, and *Mona* (Μόνα) is likely Anglesey, but there are several problems with these identifications.[141] Between *Monaoida* and *Mona* are *Adru* (῎Αδρου) and *Limnu* (Λίμνου), both described as "desolate" (ἔρημος). Pliny lists an *Andros* island between Britain and Ireland that is likely to be the same as Ptolemy's *Adru*.[142]

Ptolemy's remaining references to Ireland are short remarks that provide little new information. In his subsequent and much longer section on Britain, he refers once again to the previously named seas on Ireland's eastern and southern shores:

δυσμικῆς πλευρᾶς περιγραφὴ, ᾗ παράκειται ὅ τε ᾽Ιουερνικὸς ᾽Ωκεανὸς καὶ ὁ Οὐεργιόνιος. (*Geography* 2.2)

A description of the western coast of Britain, which faces the *Iwernikos* and *Wergionios* oceans.

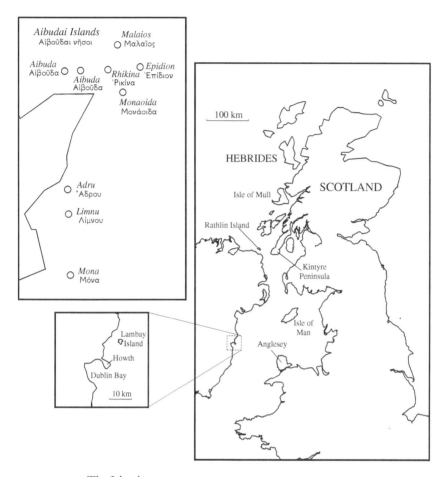

FIGURE 23. The Islands

Toward the end of his *Geography*, Ptolemy summarizes his description of the world and ranks the ten largest islands by size, from Taprobane, the greatest in his reckoning, to Britain, Ireland, and finally Cyprus in tenth place:

τῶν δὲ ἀξιολογωτέρων νήσων . . . τετάρτη δὲ τῶν Βρετανικῶν ἡ Ἰουερνία. (*Geography* 7.5)

Of the most noteworthy islands . . . the fourth is *Iwernia* of the Bretannic Isles.

In the final part of his summary, Ptolemy gives the length of days in selected positions, reminiscent of the *Almagest*, and their positions west of Alexandria:[143]

Εὐρώτης Πίναξ α'.

ὁ πρῶτος πίναξ τῆς Εὐρώπης περιέχει τὰς Βρετανικὰς νήσους. . . .

τῆς δὲ Ἰουερνίας νήσου αἱ ἐπίσημοι πόλεις· ἡ μὲν ὁμώνυμος τῇ νήσῳ πόλις Ἰουερνὶς τὴν μεγίστην ἡμέραν ἔχει ὡρῶν ἰσημερινῶν ιη ", καὶ διέστηκεν Ἀλεξανδρείας πρὸς δυσμὰς ὥραις τρισὶ καὶ τετάρτῳ. ἡ δὲ Ῥαίβα τὴν μεγάλην ἡμέραν ἔχει ὡρῶν ιη " ʟ" ιβ', καὶ διέστηκεν Ἀλεξανδρείας πρὸς δύσεις ὥραις τρισὶ καὶ πέμπτῳ. (*Geography* 8.3)

Map of Europe 1

The first map contains the Bretannic Isles. . . .

The designated cities of the island of *Iwernia*: The city of *Iwernis*, of the same name as the island, has the longest day on the summer equinox, eighteen hours. It is to the west of Alexandria three and one-quarter hours. *Rhaiba* has a long day of eighteen hours and forty-two minutes, and is to the west of Alexandria three and one-fifth hours [see Fig. 24].

Ptolemy apparently selected *Iwernis* and *Rhaiba* as having representative positions in Ireland, as both are centrally located, with *Iwernis* in the south and *Rhaiba* in the north, though not as far north on the map as the first *Rhēgia* or *Magnata*.

Apuleius

The surviving works of Apuleius (c. A.D. 125–after 170) include the *Metamorphoses* or *Golden Ass*, the only surviving Roman novel, and speeches on philosophy. He may have been the author of a translation of Pseudo-Aristotle's *De mundo* into Latin (c. A.D. 160–70):[144]

sed in altera parte orbis iacent insularum aggeres maximarum, Britanniae duae, et Albion et Hibernia, <iis> quas supra diximus [esse], maiores. (*De mundo* 7)

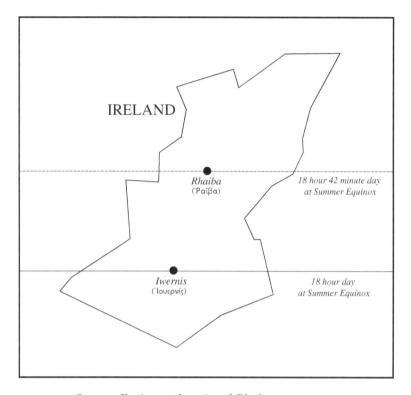

FIGURE 24. Summer Equinox at *Iwernis* and *Rhaiba*

But in the other part of the world lie the collection of the largest islands, the two Britannic Isles, *Albion* and *Hibernia*, greater than those mentioned above.

The Latin version is a close translation of the Greek and adds no new information on Ireland.

Herodian

Herodian (Aelius Herodianus), the last of the great Greek grammarians, lived and worked in Rome at the time of the emperor Marcus Aurelius. His *De prosodia catholica* (c. A.D. 160–180) was a monumental collection and commentary on the form and accentuation of tens of thousands of words, but the enormous work survives only in reduced epitome form, often with many textual problems. Three of his passages briefly mention Ireland:[145]

τὰ εἰς -ερνος Ἰταλιωτικὰ παροξύνεται, Φαλέρνος, πατέρνος, Ἰουέρνος ἔθνος ἐν τῷ πόντῳ τῷ Πρετανικῷ. (De prosodia catholica 7.175 [Lentz 1867])

The Italians provided the stimulus for the forms in *-ernos*, such as *Phalernos, paternos,* and *Iwernos,* a tribe in the Pretanic Sea.

Ἰουερνία νῆσος Πρεττανική. (De prosodia catholica 11.296 [Lentz 1867])

Iwernia, a Pretanic island.

ἔτι καὶ τὰ εἰς -νη μονογενῆ ὑπερδισύλλαβα ἔχοντα πρὸ τοῦ -ν -ρ βαρύνε-ται, Ἰέρνη νῆσος ἐν τῷ πέρατι πρὸς ταῖς δυσμαῖς, Ἰουέρνη πόλις ἐν τῷ πόντῳ τῷ Πρετανικῷ. (De prosodia catholica 12.327 [Lentz 1867])

Moreover, singular words of more than two syllables in *-ne* having an *-r* before the *-n* are accented before the *-r: Iérnē,* an island in the western edge of the world yields *Iwérnē,* a city in the Pretanic Sea.

The first passage discusses words ending in *-ernos* (-ερνος), rare in Greek, which have crept into usage by way of the languages of Italy, most especially Latin. *Iwernos* (Ἰουέρνος) is here probably an adjective used with *ethnos* (ἔθνος), "tribe," and intended to represent the plural *Iwernoi* (Ἰουέρνοι) tribe of southern Ireland noted a few years earlier by Ptolemy.[146] The context of the second passage is a list of words ending with *-nia* (-νία). The form *Iwernia* (Ἰουερνία) is identical to that found in Ptolemy, but Herodian also knows of and includes the name *Iwernē* (Ἰουέρνη) in the next passage. Herodian's final citation lists *Iwernē* (Ἰουέρνη) as a city, whereas Ptolemy has a town called *Iwernis* (Ἰουερνίς) in southern Ireland.[147]

Solinus

The *Collectanea rerum memorabilium* ("Collection of Remarkable Facts," c. A.D. 200) of Gaius Iulius Solinus was largely compiled from the earlier works of Pliny and Pomponius Mela, but it does contain some new, though dubious, information on the British Isles. Solinus' short passage on Ireland typifies this mixture of old and new material:[148]

multis insulis nec ignobilibus circumdatur, quarum Hibernia ei proximat magnitudine, inhumana incolarum ritu aspero, alias ita pabulosa, ut pecua, nisi interdum a pastibus arceantur, ad periculum agat satias. illic nullus anguis, avis rara, gens inhospita et bellicosa. sanguine interemptorum hausto prius victores vultus suos oblinunt. fas ac nefas eodem loco ducunt. apis nusquam, advectum inde pulverem seu lapillos si quis sparserit inter alvearia, examina favos deserent. sed mare quod inter hanc et Brittaniam interluit undosum inquietumque toto in anno nonnisi pauculis diebus est navigabile idque in centum viginti milia passuum latitudinis diffundi qui fidem ad verum ratiocinati sunt aestimarunt. (Collectanea rerum memorabilium 22.2–6 [Mommsen 1895])

Britain is surrounded by many significant islands, of which *Hibernia* comes closest to it in size. The latter is inhuman in the savage rituals of its inhabitants, but on the other hand is so rich in fodder that the cattle, if not removed from the fields from time to time, would happily gorge themselves to a dangerous point. On that island there are no snakes, few birds, and an unfriendly and warlike people. When the blood of killers has been drained, the victors smear it on their own faces. They treat right and wrong as the same thing. There have never been bees there, and if anyone sprinkles dust or pebbles from there among the hives, the swarms will leave the honeycombs. The sea that lies between this island and Britain is stormy and tossed during the whole year, except for a few days it is navigable. Those who have made a trustworthy measurement of the distance of this passage say it is one hundred and twenty thousand paces [c. 178 kilometers].

Solinus echoes Mela on Ireland's reportedly brutish population and fertile lands, even repeating the earlier author's statement on the dangers of overgrazing Irish cattle.[149] The Roman writer then steals the glory from St. Patrick, who, according to tradition, drove the snakes from Ireland more than two centuries later. While it is true that Ireland has no native snakes, it has long been home to bees, not to mention more than a few birds. These statements are similar to those found in Solinus' subsequent section on the British island of *Tanatus* (modern Thanet), which he also claims is without snakes, and the soil of which, he says, will kill foreign snakes when brought to any other land.[150] These statements may be partially inspired by Pliny's description of the Balearic Islands of the western Mediterranean.[151] Pliny says that soil from the island of *Ebusi* (modern

Iviza) drives away snakes, but that the nearby isle of *Colubraria* (from Latin *colubra*, "snake") is overrun by serpents and therefore very dangerous, unless the clever visitor brings along soil from *Ebusi* to repel them.[152]

The comments of Solinus on the barbaric nature of the Irish also draws on Mela's claim that the Irish were totally ignorant of civilized values, but the later writer conjures more vivid details that resemble earlier writers' descriptions of the martial nature and rituals of the continental Celts.[153] Following Pliny, Solinus comments on the distance between Britain and Ireland, but makes the passage exceedingly difficult and four times as wide as Pliny's reasonably close measurement.[154] This is in spite of the fact that Solinus claims to draw on reliable first-hand sources.

UNATTRIBUTED WORKS

Panegyric on Constantius Caesar

Almost a century separates the previous passage on Ireland by Solinus and the next reference to the island in classical literature, written in A.D. 297. This hiatus is unusually long, but it is not really surprising given the scarcity of Latin literature of any type from the third century. One reason for the lack of writings on Ireland in particular is that the tumultuous events of the era demanded a focus on internal affairs, not on poorly known islands beyond the imperial borders.[155] The Roman empire at this time endured decades of chaos that included invasions into Italy itself by the Germanic Alamanni, raids on Gaul by other German tribes, and the setting up of a separate western empire by usurpers in the latter decades of the third century. Britain also began to suffer inroads from various barbarian tribes that continued until the collapse of empire in the fifth century. A short passage from the very end of the third century breaks the long silence on Ireland, and although it supposedly refers to events of the first century B.C., the context is late-third-century Roman Britain:

> *ad hoc natio etiam tunc rudis et solis [Brittanni] Pictis modo et Hibernis adsueta hostibus adhuc seminudis, facile Romanis armis signisque cesserunt, prope ut hoc uno Caesar gloriari in illa expeditione debuerit quod navigasset Oceanum.* (*Panegyric on Constantius Caesar* 11.4 [Mynors 1964])

The Britons also, then a barbarous nation accustomed only to enemies as yet half-naked, such as the Picts and *Hiberni*, yielded easily to the arms and standards of Rome—nearly so easily that Caesar should have boasted that in that one campaign he had crossed the Ocean.

This brief reference to the *Hiberni*, or Irish, is from a panegyric praising Constantius I (the father of Constantine the Great) on the recovery of Britain for the empire. The late Latin panegyric genre is replete with flowery hyperbole, but it is at least loosely based on fact. Constantius was appointed as part of Diocletian's tetrarchy to seize northeast Gaul and Britain from the usurper Carausius, a task he skillfully accomplished. The unknown panegyric writer celebrates this recovery and compares Constantius to Julius Caesar, the first Roman general in Britain.

At the time of Caesar's invasion in the first century B.C., the writer notes, the natives of Britain were only used to dealing with inroads from other barbarians, such as the Picts and the Irish. While it is probable that earlier Britons occasionally faced these tribes during raids, we know for certain that Britain, beginning in the third century A.D., suffered repeated incursions from Picts, Irish, and others taking advantage of weakened defenses in the unstable Roman world of this era.[156] The Picts, first given this name as a whole people in this passage, were nevertheless long-time inhabitants of northern Britain who had occasionally faced and more often retreated before the Romans for centuries under individual tribal names.[157] The *Hiberni* of this passage were Irish from *Hibernia*, who here are first noted as leaving their island to harass the Romans of Britain. Hoards of Roman coins and silverware from the late imperial era unearthed in Ireland may well be evidence of such raids on Britain, but the Irish also may have been settling in Wales and along the western coast of Britain as early as this period. At the beginning of the medieval era, these Irish incursions expanded into the Irish (later called *Scotti*) settlement of large sections of north Britain, the origin of Gaelic Scotland. The Irish are rarely given a name as a whole people in Greek and Roman writings, and only here are they called *Hiberni*, a name soon superseded by the term *Scoti* or *Scotti*.[158]

Maritime Itinerary of Antonius Augustus

A Roman itinerary was the land-based equivalent of a nautical periplus. These itineraries served the very practical purpose of familiarizing a Roman army commander with the land through which he marched, including distances and road conditions. Among the surviving itineraries is the

Antonine Itinerary (*Itinerarium provinciarum Antonini Augusti*, c. late third century A.D.), which details over two hundred marches throughout the Roman empire, from Britain to Africa. Affixed to the end of this document is a *Maritime Itinerary* (*Itinerarium maritimum*) in the old periplus tradition that gives distances and lists islands in the Mediterranean and Atlantic. After giving routes and distances along the Italian and Gaulish coasts, the *Maritime Itinerary* lists a few islands around Britain:

> *item in mari Oceano, quod Gallias et*
> *Brittanias interluit:*
> *insul[a]e Orcades numero III*
> *insula Clota in Hiverione.*
> (*Maritime Itinerary* 508.3–509.1 [Cuntz 1929])

> Also in the Ocean sea that flows
> between the Gauls and the Brittanic Isles:
> the *Orcades* islands, three in number,
> the island *Clota* in the *Hiverione* Sea.

The misplacement of the Orkneys and other islands in the sea between Gaul and Britain does not inspire confidence in the accuracy or textual transmission of this section of the *Itinerary*, and indeed, the passage as it survives is problematic. Mela and Ptolemy number the Orkneys at thirty (XXX), which Orosius expands to thirty-three (XXXIII).[159] The three (III) *Orcades* here may be a corruption of either tradition. The line *insula Clota in Hiverione* is even more puzzling. It may intend two islands, an *insula Clota* (variant *Glota*) and an abbreviated *in(sula) Hiverione* (variant *Iverione*), or an island *Clota* in the *Hiverione* or Irish Sea (preposition *in* plus object). In any event, the supposed island *Clota* is probably a misreading of the Scottish river name *Clota* (the Clyde) labeled on the sea on a source map and taken by the *Itinerary* author for an island.[160] The abbreviation *in* for *in(sula)* is possible, but it does not occur elsewhere in the *Maritime Itinerary* in spite of ample opportunities, whereas *in* as a preposition used to describe the placement of an island in a sea occurs several times.[161] In the final reading, all that can be reasonably taken from this passage is a late-third-century variation on the name for Ireland, *Hiverione*.[162]

Panegyric on Constantine Augustus

An anonymous panegyric of A.D. 310 is addressed to Constantine the Great and praises the military actions of his father Constantius I in Britain:[163]

> *neque enim ille tot tantisque rebus gestis non dico Calidonum aliorumque Pictorum silvas et paludes, sed nec Hiberniam proximam nec Thylen ultimam nec ipsas, si quae sunt, Fortunatorum insulas dignabatur adquirere.*
> (*Panegyric on Constantine Augustus* 7.2 [Mynors 1964])

Nor do I say that he, even with so many great and various deeds accomplished, deemed worthy of conquest the forests and swamps of the Calidonians and other Picts, nor nearby *Hibernia* nor furthest Thule nor, if they exist, the Isles of the Blessed.

Constantius recovered Britain for the empire in A.D. 296 and returned to the island in 305 to conduct campaigns against the Picts in northern Britain. His son Constantine joined him there just before his father's death in 306 and was proclaimed Augustus (one of two dual emperors) by the local legions, though it was several years before the rank was officially recognized.

Constantius had no interest in occupying the remote highlands of the Calidonians and other Pictish tribes after their defeat; he merely wanted to discourage future Pictish incursions into Roman Britain. The panegyrist acknowledges that it was Constantius' lack of interest that prevented such an occupation, not any absence of military skill or ability. The oration reinforces this point by proclaiming that he moreover had no desire to conquer other increasingly distant and hypothetical lands, such as nearby Ireland, Thule, or the mythical Isles of the Blessed.[164] This is the first reference since Tacitus to any potential Roman military threat to Ireland—a threat that, as in Agricola's time two centuries before, was viewed as minimal at least at this date, since Ireland was not deemed worthy of invasion by Constantius, or at least by the flowery oratory of the unknown writer.[165] However, the threat to Roman Britain from the Irish was soon to increase, as noted in the following passages.

Nomina provinciarum omnium

The *Nomina provinciarum omnium* ("Names of All the Provinces," c. A.D. 312) is a short list of the divisions and provinces of the Roman empire. Appended to this list is a brief section naming forty tribes that were a growing threat to the empire, including the *Scoti*, a new term for the Irish:

> *gentes barbarae quae pullulaverunt sub imperatoribus: Scoti, Picti, Caledonii. . . . (Nomina provinciarum omnium* 13 [Riese 1878])
>
> Barbarian tribes who have increased under the emperors: *Scoti*, Picts, Caledonians. . . .

The earlier panegyric on Constantius first suggested the threat to Roman Britain by the Picts and the Irish *Hiberni*, but beginning with the *Nomina provinciarum omnium*, the name *Hiberni* was replaced by *Scoti* (alternately spelled *Scotti*).[166] This usage would continue in classical literature until the end of the empire and beyond.

The identification of the *Scoti* with the Irish is clear from classical and later records. As noted, the *Panegyric on Constantius Caesar,* written perhaps fifteen years before the *Nomina provinciarum omnium,* pairs the Picts and the *Hiberni,* clearly referring to the Irish.[167] The *Panegyric on Constantine Augustus* of 310 continues to group together the land of the Picts and *Hibernia,* also adding Thule and the Isles of the Blessed.[168] But beginning here in the *Nomina provinciarum omnium,* the Picts, as a threat to Roman Britain, are paired with the *Scoti* and occasionally others; never again do we find in classical literature Picts and *Hiberni* grouped together.[169] Thus it seems that the equation "Picts and *Hiberni*" was replaced in the early fourth century by "Picts and *Scot(t)i.*" This change in itself does not prove that the *Scoti* were Irish, but several statements in late classical writers show that at least these contemporary authors believed the two were one and the same. Jerome places the homeland of the *Scotti* "near the Britons" (*de Brittannorum vincinia*), whereas Claudian says plainly that Ireland (*Hiverne*) wept at the mounds of dead *Scotti* slain by the grandfather of the emperor Honorius.[170] Claudian also claims that the *Scotti* "roused all *Hiverne*" in response to the Roman general Stilicho.[171] Early medieval writers working in the classical tradition also identify Ireland as the land of the *Scotti,* such as the fifth-century writer Prosper Tiro, who says that in the year 431, the pope sent the missionary Palladius to Ireland "to the *Scotti* believing in Christ" (*ad Scottos in Christum credentes*), and the early-seventh-century bishop Isidorus of Seville, who plainly states that *Scotia* and Ireland were the same.[172]

The identity of the *Scoti* as Irish is secure, but the reasons for the change of names from *Hibernia/Hiberni* to *Scotia/Scoti* and the origin of the term *Scoti* are uncertain. It cannot be a coincidence that the terminology changed just as Roman Britain was first being threatened by Irish raiders. Previously most of the classical world, if they thought of the Irish at all, viewed them as a distant tribe at the edge of the world. But suddenly the Britons and others in the northwestern part of the empire were meeting the Irish face-to-face as they raided their farms and towns, killing and wrecking havoc all around. The name may have been transferred by frightened Romans to the Irish as a whole from a group of Irish raiders who called themselves *Scoti*, perhaps from the suitably sinister root **skot-* ("darkness"), also found in Greek *skotos* (σκότος, "darkness, gloom"). But any etymology is speculative and complicated by the fact that names based on *Scot-* were popular in Celtic names from Gaulish inscriptions predating references to the Irish *Scoti* by centuries.[173]

Orphic Argonautica

The voyage of Jason and the Argonauts is one of the earliest and most enduring Greek tales. Poets from Homer to Pindar and Callimachus wrote of the voyage to Colchis in the eastern Black Sea to retrieve the Golden Fleece and the homeward journey of heroes such as Hercules, Theseus, and Orpheus. Versions of the story, especially concerning the return voyage, grew more diverse and elaborate as the centuries passed, with the Argonauts eventually sailing through the rivers of Europe or into the northern ocean on their way back to Greece. A late version of the tale, from the late fourth century A.D., has Orpheus narrating the story as the ship Argo (the speaker of the first passage) sails near Ireland:[174]

> νῦν γὰρ δὴ λυγρῆς τε καὶ ἀργαλέης κακότητος
> λήξομαι, εἰ νήσοισιν Ἰερνίσιν ἆσσον ἴκωμαι.
> (*Orphic Argonautica* 1165–66)

> For now wretched and grievous misery
> will be my lot, if I come near the islands of *Iernē*.

A few lines later, the helmsman Ancaius successfully steers the ship forward on its harrowing journey:

> Ἀγκαῖος δ' οἴακας ἐπισταμένως ἐτίταινε,
> πὰρ δ' ἄρα νῆσον ἄμειβον Ἰερνίδα. (*Orphic Argonautica* 1180–81)

Ancaius expertly held the rudder,
passing then near the isle of *Iernē*.

The Orphic poet is here surprisingly confused about the Britannic Isles, which would include Britain, Ireland, and the surrounding smaller islands, and renames them all the Irish Isles.

Pacatus

The Gallic orator Latinius Pacatus Drepanius celebrated the victory of the emperor Theodosius I over the usurper Magnus Maximus on the occasion of a visit by Theodosius to Rome in A.D. 389. In the panegyric, Pacatus praised Theodosius Flavius, the father of Theodosius I, for his recovery of Britain from the Saxons, Picts, and *Scoti* in A.D. 367:[175]

> *attritam pedestribus proeliis Britanniam referam? Saxo consumptus bellis navalibus offeretur. redactum ad palades suas Scotum loquar? (Panegyric on Theodosius 5.2)*
>
> Shall I tell how Britain was worn down by infantry battles? The Saxon defeated in naval battles is an example. Shall I speak of the *Scoti* driven back to their own swamps?

Theodosius Flavius arrived in southern Britain and drove back the marauding barbarians to reestablish Roman rule in the area, recovering and returning most of the booty stolen from the Britons.[176] The reference to the *Scoti* "driven back to their own swamps" could imply Roman naval action against the Irish *Scoti* as well as against the Saxons, but even so it would not necessarily mean that Roman troops followed the *Scoti* into the Irish Sea or to Ireland. Claudian intriguingly speaks of Theodosius Flavius in the same campaign pursuing the *Scoti* afar and sailing the Hyperborean Ocean (which Ptolemy places off Ireland's northern coast); but the panegyric genre frequently employs hyperbole and exaggeration.[177] Nevertheless, Roman military action on the Irish Sea and even reaching into Ireland at this time cannot be totally ruled out.

Ammianus Marcellinus

Ammianus Marcellinus (c. A.D. 330–95) was the last of the great Roman historians. His *History* (c. A.D. 392), much of which is now lost, deals with events from the close of the first century A.D. until the late fourth century. The sections covering the period of his own adult life are the most detailed and important, as Ammianus was closely associated with many major political and military figures of the time and had himself traveled throughout the empire with the Roman armies. Three of his passages mention raids by the Irish *Scotti;* two also are the first to note the *Attacotti*, who may have originated in Ireland as well:

> *consulatu vero Constantii deciens, terque Iuliani, in Britanniis cum Scottorum Pictorumque gentium ferarum excursus, rupta quiete condicta, loca limitibus vicina vastarent, et implicaret formido provincias, praeteritarum cladium congerie fessas.* (*History* 20.1.1)

But in Britain during the tenth consulship of Constantius and the third of Julian, raids by savage tribes of *Scotti* and Picts broke the arranged peace and devastated the frontier regions. Terror filled the provincials, worn down as they were by the frequent calamities of the past.

> *hoc tempore velut per universum orbem Romanum, bellicum canentibus bucinis, excitae gentes saevissimae, limites sibi proximos persultabant. Gallias Raetiasque simul Alamanni populabantur . . . Picti Saxonesque et Scotti, et Attacotti Britannos aerumnis vexavere continuis.* (*History* 26.4.5)

At that time, as if war trumpets were sounding throughout the whole Roman world, the most savage tribes were roused and poured across the frontiers nearest to them. While the Alamanni were ravaging Gaul and Raetia . . . the Picts, Saxons, *Scotti*, and *Attacotti* were harassing the Britons with constant troubles.

> *illud tamen sufficiet dici, quod eo tempore Picti in duas gentes divisi, Dicalydonas et Verturiones, itidemque Attacotti, bellicosa hominum natio, et Scotti, per diversa vagantes, multa populabantur.* (*History* 27.8.5)

Suffice it to say, however, that at that time the Picts, divided into the two tribes of the Dicalydones and Verturiones, as well as the warlike nation of the *Attacotti* and the *Scotti*, were roaming far and wide, ravaging many lands.

During the mid-fourth century A.D., the western part of the empire had suffered numerous incursions by Germanic tribes, whereas Britain had only endured minor raids from barbarian tribes within the British Isles. But in 360, as noted in the first passage, the Picts and Scots launched a large-scale attack against the Roman Britons. The soon-to-be emperor Julian, later known as "the Apostate," sent a force from Gaul under his commander Lupicinus to respond to the attack, though the exact outcome is unknown. But four years later, the second passage records that the situation had declined even further. The Germanic Alamanni were attacking Gaul and alpine Raetia, while the Picts and Scots were still harassing the Britons. To make matters worse, they had now been joined by Saxon raiders from northern Germany and a people known as the *Attacotti*.

The origins of these *Attacotti* (*Atticoti* and *Atecotti* in other works) are largely mysterious, but it is at least possible that they were originally from Ireland. One reason for thinking this is that they are usually paired with the Irish *Scotti*—but then, so are the Picts from northern Britain and the Saxons from across the North Sea.[178] Also, they are confused with the *Scotti* in different manuscripts of one passage from Jerome.[179] However, these are not compelling reasons to place the *Attacotti* homeland in Ireland, though other areas from which these previously unknown marauders could have originated are limited given the geography and logistics of launching raids on Roman Britain. If they were Irish, it is interesting to note that the *Notitia dignitatum* of about A.D. 395 lists *Atecotti* auxiliaries serving in the Roman legions in Italy, Gaul, and Illyria.[180]

Just three years later, the third passage relates that the Picts (composed of two groups), *Scotti*, and *Attacotti* had expanded their activities even further. These tribes were ravaging Roman Britain south to the London area but were driven back by Theodosius Flavius, who recovered Britain for Rome.[181] The extent of their raiding "many lands" beyond Britain is unclear, but Jerome speaks of *Atticoti* or *Scoti* harassing the countryfolk of northeastern Gaul during roughly the same period.[182]

UNATTRIBUTED WORKS
Historia Augusta

In contrast to the dire picture of the late fourth century presented by Ammianus, the author of the imperial biography of Marcus Claudius Tacitus in the *Historia Augusta*, writing in the late fourth century A.D. of events in the late third century, speaks not of defending the borders of the empire, but of expanding them to include even Ireland:[183]

> *quo tempore responsum est ab haruspicibus quandocumque ex eorum familia imperatorem Romanum futurum seu per feminam seu per virum, qui det iudices Parthis ac Persis, qui Francos et Alamannos sub Romanis legibus habeat, qui per omnem Africam barbarum non relinquat, qui Taprobanis praesidem imponat, qui ad Iuvernam insulam proconsulem mittat, qui Sarmatis omnibus iudicet, qui terram omnem, qua Oceano ambitur, captis omnibus gentibus suam faciat. (Historia Augusta—Tacitus 15.2)*

At this time it was foretold by the soothsayers that in due time there would be a Roman emperor from their family, through either the female or the male line, who would select judges for the Parthians and Persians, who would bring the Franks and Alamanni under Roman law, who would not leave behind a barbarian in all of Africa, who would install a governor in Taprobane and send a proconsul to the island of *Iuverna*, who would be a judge for all the Sarmatians, and who, with all the tribes conquered, would make his own all the lands that the Ocean embraces.

After the death of the emperor Aurelian in A.D. 275, Tacitus ruled for six months before being murdered by his own troops. His brother Marcus Annius Florianus succeeded him, reigning for only two months before likewise being killed by his own troops. Nevertheless, these two mediocre emperors had statues erected to them by their numerous children and relatives on the family lands just north of Rome. True to their luck, both statues were shattered into fragments by lightning. The local soothsayers were, however, quick to interpret this omen positively; they uttered the above prophecy, wisely adding the disclaimer that this future emperor would not come for a thousand years. *Iuverna* (Ireland), to be ruled by a proconsular governor, and Taprobane (Sri Lanka) are here used figuratively as two lands on opposite ends of the known world.

Pseudo-Hegesippus

A fourth- or fifth-century writer, taking the name of the second-century Church historian Hegesippus, translated and condensed the *Jewish War* of Josephus from Greek into Latin. A speech on the power of Rome, though set centuries before events of the late fourth century A.D., refers to Ireland:

> *quid attexam Britannias, interfuso mari a toto orbe divisas, et a Romanis in orbem terrarum redactas? tremit hos Scotia, quae terris nihil debet.*
> (Pseudo-Hegesippus, *Jewish War* 5.15)

> Why should I mention the Britannic Isles, separated from the whole world by the wide sea, and yet restored to the world by the Romans? *Scotia*, which owes loyalty to no one, fears them.

Ireland is here for the first and only time in classical literature called *Scotia* ("land of the *Scotti*"), a term later transferred to northern Britain.

Jerome

Eusebius Hieronymus, better known as Jerome, was born into a Christian family in Dalmatia on the Adriatic coast opposite Italy around A.D. 347 and educated at Rome. As a young man, he sought his worldly fortune at the imperial court at Augusta Treverorum in northeastern Gaul, but he was there influenced by Christian asceticism. He journeyed to the east, eventually settling in Bethlehem. There he learned Greek and Hebrew, which he put to good use as the translator of the Vulgate, the standard Latin Bible for many centuries. Jerome was unusual among the early Church fathers as a first-rank scholar with an impressive command of classical literature. But he was also a passionate soul devoted to Christian doctrine and monastic ideals. Aside from the Vulgate Bible, his works include histories, dictionaries, biblical commentaries, polemical treatises, and letters.

Several passages from his works mention the *Scot(t)i* (Jerome uses both spellings) and *Atticoti*, including an alleged eyewitness account of cannibalism in a work defending virginity and monasticism:

*quid loquar de caeteris nationibus, cum ipse adolescentulus in Gallia Atti-
cotos (al. Scotos), gentem Britannicam, humanis vesci carnibus: et cum per
silvas porcorum greges et armentorum pecudumque reperiant, pastorum
nates et feminarum, et papillas solere abscindere, et has solas ciborum deli-
cias arbitrari? Scotorum natio uxores proprias non habet: et quasi Platonis politiam legerit, et Catonis sectetur exemplum, nulla apud eos coniux
propia est, sed ut cuique libitum fuerit, pecudum more lasciviunt. (Adversus Jovinianum 2.7)*

Why should I speak of other nations when I myself as a young man
in Gaul saw the *Atticoti* [or *Scoti*], a British people, feeding on human
flesh? Moreover, when they come across herds of pigs and cattle in
the forests, they frequently cut off the buttocks of the shepherds and
their wives, and their nipples, regarding these alone as delicacies. The
nation of the *Scoti* do not have individual wives, but, as if they had
read Plato's *Republic* or followed the example of Cato, no wife belongs
to a particular man, but as each desires, they indulge themselves like
beasts.

Jerome uses these *Atticoti* or *Scoti*, depending on the manuscript, as the
antithesis of Christian ideals of self-restraint. His residence in Augusta
Treverorum (modern Trier) probably included the year (A.D. 367) for
which Ammianus Marcellinus reports a concerted attack by the *Scotti*, *Attacotti*, and other tribes on Britain, when these groups were ranging far and
wide in many lands (see Fig. 25).[184] Thus their presence in Gaul is cred-
ible, though it is remarkable to think of an Irish presence far from home in
such an important Roman province.[185] Jerome's *Atticoti* or *Scoti*, however,
may not have been raiders, especially as Jerome himself could approach
them without losing his own body parts. As noted earlier, according to the
Notitia dignitatum of the late fourth century, there were *Atecotti* auxiliaries
serving in the Roman army in Gaul and as far away as Illyria.[186] There is
also the possibility that what Jerome witnessed was not genuine cannibalism at all, but some rough-and-ready foreign soldiers having fun with a
gullible Roman youth over a meal of mutton stew.[187]

The charge that the *Scotti* trade women freely among themselves is
also found in one of Jerome's letters:

*sed Scottorum et Atticotorum ritu, ac de Republica Platonis, promiscuas
uxores, communes liberos habeant. (Epistle 69.415)*

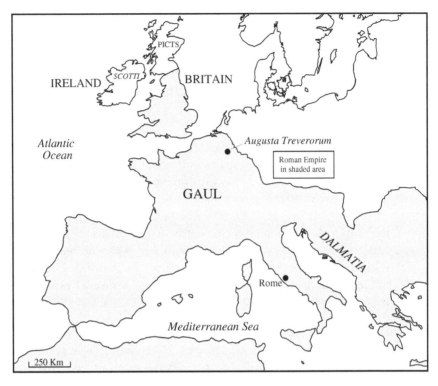

FIGURE 25. The Roman Empire at the Time of Jerome (b. A.D. 347)

But in the manner of the *Scotti* and *Atticoti*, and the *Republic* of Plato, let them have wives enjoyed by all and children in common.

This is reminiscent of the lack of Irish morality alleged earlier in Pomponius Mela and Solinus.[188] Jerome may also have been influenced by Caesar's description of polygamy among the Britons.[189]

In another letter, Jerome notes that before the introduction of Christianity, no barbarian nation, including the *Scotti*, knew of the revealed truth of God as found in Jewish tradition:

> *Deus ab Adam usque ad Moysen, et a Moyse usque ad adventum Christi passus sit universas gentes perire ignorantia Legis et mandatorum Dei. neque enim Britannia fertilis provincia tyrannorum, et Scoticae gentes, omnesque usque ad Oceanum per circuitum barbarae nationes Moysen Prophetasque cognoverant. (Epistle 123.1038)*

God, from Adam to Moses and from Moses to the coming of Christ, allowed all the nations to perish ignorant of the Law and his instructions. For neither Britain, fertile province of tyrants, nor the *Scotti*, nor any throughout the barbarian nations to the Ocean knew Moses and the Prophets.

The final two passages of Jerome show his temperamental side as he uncharitably describes an unnamed critic, who almost certainly can be identified with his influential rival Pelagius:

> *ut nuper indoctus calumniator erupit, qui Commentarios meos in Epistulam Pauli ad Ephesios reprehendendos putat . . . nec recordatur stolidissimus et Scottorum pultibus praegravatus nos in ipso dixisse opere. . . . (Commentary on Jeremiah* 1 [prologue])

> Recently an ignorant petty critic has burst forth, who thinks that my commentaries on the *Epistle of Paul to the Ephesians* should be condemned . . . nor does that most stupid man, weighed down with *Scotti* porridge, recall that I said in the very same work. . . .

> *ipseque mutus latrat per Alpinum canem, grandem et corpulentum et, qui calcibus magis possit saevire quam dentibus. habet enim progeniem Scotticae gentis de Brittannorum vicinia. (Commentary on Jeremiah* 3 [prologue])

> Though [Satan] himself is silent, he barks through an Alpine dog, large and fat, who is able to lash out more with his heels than with his teeth. His lineage is of the *Scotti* people near the Britons.

Pelagius (c. A.D. 354–after 418) by no means abandoned the major traditions of Christianity, but he did reject the contemporary views on virginity and original sin and emphasized the ability of an individual believer to rise above moral weakness through his or her own efforts. These arguments provoked the anger of Augustine as well as Jerome and earned Pelagius many enemies among the Church hierarchy. Jerome clearly associates him with the *Scotti*, but other sources record that he was British-born. This is not necessarily a contradiction, as there were probably established Irish settlements in Britain at this time. But it is also possible, given the level of venom in these passages, that Jerome was simply looking for the most insulting label possible related to the British Isles, with *Scottus* yielding the maximum insult, especially noting the way in which Jerome describes the *Scotti* in his earlier writings.

Prudentius

Aurelius Clemens Prudentius (A.D. 348–after 405) was the greatest of the Christian Latin poets and was very influential in the medieval period. His *Apotheosis* (c. A.D. 390–95) urges the reader to acknowledge the existence of God and accept the divinity of Christ:

> *non recipit natura hominis, modo quadrupes ille*
> *non sit, et erecto spectet caelestia vultu,*
> *non recipit neget ut regimen pollere supremum.*
> *istud et ipse Numae tacitus sibi sensit haruspex,*
> *semifer et Scottus sentit, cane milite peior. (Apotheosis 212–16)*

> Human nature, unless one is four-footed beast,
> with face uplifted to the sky,
> cannot deny that a supreme order rules.
> Even Numa's diviner felt this in his heart,
> as does the half-wild *Scottus*, worse than a war-hound.

Prudentius sees the existence of a divine order as acknowledged by all people of the world, whether civilized pagans such as the diviners of the early Roman king Numa or even the barbaric *Scotti*, only slightly better than four-footed beasts.

Symmachus

Quintus Aurelius Symmachus (c. A.D. 340–402), a Roman senator and orator, was one of the last great defenders of traditional Roman religion against the increasingly dominant voice of Christian emperors and politicians. His many surviving letters to over a hundred correspondents include a short note to his close friend Flavianus (c. A.D. 393) in which he mentions recent arrivals in Rome from the north:

> *ut nunc septem Scotticorum canum probavit oblatio, quos praelusionis die*
> *ita Roma mirata est, ut ferreis caveis putaret advectos. (Epistle 2.77)*

As now the presentation of seven *Scotti* dogs has demonstrated, which on the day of the prelude so astonished Rome, that it was thought they were brought in iron cages.

Canines from the British Isles were not a new trade item in the Roman world. Strabo included hunting dogs among the principal exports of Britain in the first century A.D., along with metals, cattle, and slaves.[190] Later classical writers also mention British hounds, noting that they are not very large and certainly not handsome, but are exceedingly fast and strong.[191]

The seven *Scotti* dogs brought to Rome were presented to the astonished crowd on the day of a prelude (*praelusio*) to public games, suggesting the dogs were to play some role in entertaining the Roman populace.

Servius

The grammarian and Virgilian commentator Servius, writing in the late fourth century A.D., briefly mentions Ireland while explaining a passage from Virgil's *Georgics:*

> *THULE insula est Oceani inter septemtrionalem et occidentalem plagam, ultra Britanniam, Hiberniam, Orcadas.* (*Commentary on Virgil's Georgics* 1.30)

> THULE is an island in the Ocean between the northern and western region, beyond Britain, *Hibernia*, and the *Orcades.*

Virgil's line celebrates that Augustus might someday rule as a god over vast and distant lands, including *ultima Thule* ("farthest Thule"), soon to be a proverbial expression for the most distant place on earth. Servius, however, takes a more literal and traditional approach and explains this reference by saying that Thule is an island in the far north, beyond even Britain, Ireland, and the Orkney Islands. Strabo also places Thule to the north of Ireland.[192]

Claudian

Claudius Claudianus (c. A.D. 370–c. A.D. 404) was an Alexandrian Greek who came to Rome as a young man and rapidly became renowned for praising men of power, notably the emperor Honorius and his powerful minister

Stilicho. His panegyric poetry, as is common in the genre, is marked by hyperbole and frequent use of speeches. Four of Claudian's works mention the *Scotti* and Ireland, the first two in his speeches of 396 and 398 praising the weak ruler Honorius, but referring to actions by Honorius' grandfather, Theodosius Flavius, several decades earlier:

> *ille leves Mauros nec falso nomine Pictos*
> *edomuit Scottumque vago mucrone secutus*
> *fregit Hyperboreas remis audacibus undas.* (*Panegyric on the Third*
> *Consulship of the Emperor Honorius 54–56*)

He conquered the swift Moors and the well-named Picts,
and following the *Scotti* with his wandering sword,
he broke the Hyperborean waves with his daring oars.

> *quid rigor aeternus, caeli quid frigora prosunt*
> *ignotumque fretum? maduerunt Saxone fuso*
> *Orcades; incaluit Pictorum sanguine Thyle;*
> *Scottorum cumulos flevit glacialis Hiverne.* (*Panegyric on the Fourth*
> *Consulship of the Emperor Honorius 8.30–33*)

What endless cold, what wintry air, what unknown sea
could affect him? The Orkneys were soaked in Saxon gore;
Thule was warmed by Pictish blood;
icy *Hiverne* wept at the mounds of dead *Scotti*.

This is the same campaign for the recovery of Britain in 367 noted earlier by Ammianus Marcellinus and Pacatus.[193] As noted under the discussion of Pacatus, these references indicate that the Romans possibly, though not necessarily, engaged in naval action against Ireland itself during this sweeping action against the *Scotti*. The second passage is also the earliest reference directly connecting Ireland (*Hiverne*) and the *Scotti*, though it falls just short of saying, as does Orosius a few years later, that Ireland is the homeland of the *Scotti*.[194] Claudian, presumably for poetic effect, also resurrects the long-outdated notion that Ireland was cold and icy.[195] Moreover, Claudian's unlikely references to Romans slaying Saxons in the Orkney Islands and Picts in near-mythical Thule cast some doubt on the historicity of the Irish weeping for the fallen *Scotti* after Theodosius Flavius' campaign. Still, since we know the *Scotti* who were ravaging Britain in 367 were beaten back by the Romans, and since we can reasonably assume they originated in Ireland, Claudian's poetic portrait of mourning in Ireland should not be dismissed, even if the descriptions of Saxons and Picts suffer from geographical hyperbole.

In a minor poem, an *epithalamium* ("wedding song") of perhaps A.D. 399, Claudian celebrates the marriage of his friend Palladius to Celerina, whose father was an important official Roman military commander who decided:

> *quae Sarmaticis custodia ripis,*
> *quae saevis obiecta Getis, quae Saxona frenat*
> *vel Scottum legio. . . . (Epithalamium of Palladius and Celerina* 88–90)

which legion should protect the Sarmatian shores,
and oppose the savage Geti, which to restrain
the Saxon and *Scottus. . . .*

In the year 400, Claudian composed a panegyric for Honorius' general and father-in-law Stilicho, the power behind the throne in the western empire for more than a decade:

> *inde Caledonio velata Britannia monstro,*
> *ferro picta genas, cuius vestigia verrit*
> *caerulus Oceanique aestum mentitur amictus:*
> *"me quoque vicinis pereuntem gentibus" inquit*
> *"munivit Stilicho, totam cum Scottus Hivernen*
> *movit et infesto spumavit remige Tethys.*
> *illius effectum curis, ne tela timerem*
> *Scottica, ne Pictum tremerem, ne litore toto*
> *prospicerem dubiis venturum Saxona ventis."*
> (*On Stilicho's Consulship* 2.247–55)

Then Britain spoke, covered in the skin of a Caledonian beast,
painted cheeks etched with tattoos,
blue cloak like the swell of the sea sweeping to her feet:
"Stilicho also defended me when I was perishing
from neighboring tribes, when the *Scottus* roused all
Hiverne and the sea foamed with hostile oars.
Due to his care, I do not fear the spears of the *Scotti,*

nor tremble at the Pict, nor watch along my whole coast
for the Saxon coming on uncertain winds."

Personified Britain, here looking oddly like a Pict, steps forward to thank
Stilicho for Roman protection against *Scotti*, Picts, and Saxons. Assuming
there is some basis in fact for this praise poem, the nature of this defense
(whether a campaign, reinforcements, or fortifications), the date or dates,
and whether Stilicho himself was present in Britain are all unknown. But
Claudian again links Ireland and the *Scotti* in even stronger terms and con-
tends that Britain was made safe thanks to the leadership of Stilicho.

Soon thereafter, however, Claudian describes the withdrawal from
Britain of Roman troops to defend the core of the empire against the
Gothic invasion of Italy under Alaric in 402:

> *enit et extremis legio praetenta Britannis,*
> *quae Scotto dat frena truci ferroque notatas*
> *perlegit exanimes Picto moriente figuras.* (*Gothic War* 416–18)

Then comes the legion protecting distant Britain,
which restrains the fierce *Scottus* and surveyed
the strange figures tattooed on the dying Pict.

The removal of these troops did not result in the immediate collapse of Roman power in Britain, but it did promote political instability and weaken
the defenses of the island to the point that soon thereafter, Britain was
effectively no longer under Roman control.

Marcianus

Marcianus composed a periplus of the seas surrounding the Mediterranean world, including measurements of coastlines and some inland areas.
Written at perhaps the beginning of the fifth century A.D., his *Periplus*
provides little new information and sometimes distorts its earlier sources,
most notably Ptolemy, on Ireland and other lands.

Marcianus begins by ranking the islands of the world, including Ireland, as did many geographers before him:[196]

> τῶν δὲ μεγίστων νήσων ἢ χερσονήσων, καὶ τῆς πρώτης τάξεως, πρώτη
> μὲν ἡ Ταπροβάνη νῆσος ἡ Παλαισιμούνδου καλουμένη πρότερον, νῦν δὲ

Σαλική· δευτέρα δὲ τῶν Πρεττανικῶν ἡ Ἀλβίων, τρίτη δὲ ἡ Χρυσῆ χερ-
σόνησος, τετάρτη δὲ τῶν Πρεττανικῶν ἡ Ἰουερνία. (*Periplus of the Outer
Sea* 1.8)

Of the largest islands and peninsulas of the first rank, the first is the
island Taprobane, once called *Palaisimoundou*, but now *Salike*; the
second is *Albion* of the Prettanic Isles, the third the Golden *Cherso-
nese*, the fourth *Iwernia* of the Prettanic Isles.

Taprobane (Sri Lanka) ranks first, followed by Britain, then the *chersonesos*
(literally "land-island") of the Malay peninsula, with Ireland fourth.

The *Periplus* proper begins by listing the areas to be covered, including Ireland and Britain; then, after surveying the coastal areas of continental Europe, Marcianus describes the British Isles:[197]

τάδε ἔνεστιν ἐν τῷ β΄ Μαρκιανοῦ περίπλῳ ἑῴου καὶ ἑσπερίου ὠκεανοῦ.
. . . περὶ τῶν Πρεττανικῶν νήσων.
Ἰουερνίας νήσου Πρεττανικῆς περίπλους.
Ἀλβίωνος νήσου Πρεττανικῆς περίπλους.

περὶ τῶν Πρεττανικῶν νήσων.

αἱ Πρεττανικαὶ νῆσοι δύο εἰσίν, ἥ τε καλουμένη Ἀλβίων καὶ ἡ Ἰουερνία.
ἀλλ᾽ ἡ μὲν Ἀλβίων μείζων κατὰ πολὺ τυγχάνει. . . . ἡ δὲ ἑτέρα νῆσος ἡ
Ἰουερνία ὑπὲρ αὐτὴν κειμένη, δυτικωτέρα δὲ τυγχάνουσα, ἐλάσσων τέ
ἐστι τῷ μεγέθει, καὶ τὴν ἴσην ἔχει θέσιν τῇ προειρημένῃ. ταύτης τοίνυν
τῆς προτέρας τὸν περίπλουν ἀναγράψομεν, εἶθ᾽ οὕτως ἐπὶ τὴν μείζονα
ἐλευσόμεθα.

Ἰουερνίας νήσου Πρεττανικῆς περίπλους.

ἡ Ἰουερνία νῆσος ἡ Πρεττανικὴ περιορίζεται ἀπὸ μὲν τῶν ἄρκτων τῷ
ὑπερκειμένῳ καὶ καλουμένῳ Ὑπερβορείῳ ὠκεανῷ, ἀπὸ δὲ ἀνατολῶν τῷ
ὠκεανῷ τῷ καλουμένῳ Ἰουερνικῷ, ἀπὸ δὲ δυσμῶν τῷ δυτικῷ ὠκεανῷ,
ἀπὸ δὲ μεσημβρίας τῷ καλουμένῳ Οὐεργιουίῳ ὠκεανῷ. Καὶ ἡ μὲν ὅλη
θέσις τῆς νήσου τοῦτον ἔχει τὸν τρόπον. . . .

ἔστι δὲ τῆς Ἰουερνίας νήσου τῆς Πρεττανικῆς τὸ μὲν μῆκος μέγιστον
ἀπὸ τοῦ Νοτίου ἀκρωτηρίου ἀρχόμενον, καὶ καταλῆγον ἐπὶ τὸ
Ῥοβόγδιον ἄκρον, ὡς εἶναι τῆς νήσου τὸ μῆκος σταδίων ,βρο΄. τὸ δὲ
πλάτος ἄρχεται μὲν ἀπὸ τοῦ Ἱεροῦ ἄκρου, περαιοῦται δὲ εἰς τὸ

Ῥοβόγδιον ἄκρον, ὡς εἶναι τῆς νήσου τὸ πλάτος σταδίων ͵αωλδ΄. τὰ δὲ
ἄκρα αὐτῆς ἀπὸ τῶν ὁριζόντων διέστηκε τὸν τρόπον τοῦτον· τὸ μὲν
ἀρκτῷον αὐτῆς ἄκρον ἀπὸ τοῦ ἀρκτῴου ὁρίζοντος σταδίους ͵α,δσν΄· τὸ
δὲ δυτικὸν αὐτῆς ἄκρον . . . ἀπὸ τῆς ἰσημερίας σταδίους ͵͵γ,ητιζ΄ · τὸ δὲ
ἀνατολικὸν ἀπὸ τῆς ἀνατολῆς σταδίους ͵͵δ τιζ΄ · ἔχει δὲ ἔθνη ις΄, πόλεις
ἐπισήμους ια΄, ποταμοὺς ἐπισήμους ιε΄, ἀκρωτήρια ἐπίσημα ε΄, νήσους
ἐπισήμους ϛ΄. οἱ πάντες τοῦ περίπλου τῆς Ἰουερνίας οὐ πλεῖον σταδίων
͵θπε΄, οὐχ ἧττον σταδίων ͵ϛωμε΄.

Ἀλβίωνος νήσου Πρεττανικῆς περίπλους

ἡ Ἀλβίων νῆσος ἡ Πρεττανικὴ περιορίζεται . . . ἀπὸ δὲ δύσεως τῷ τε
Ἰουερνικῷ ὠκεανῷ, μεθ᾽ ὃν ἡ Ἰουερνία νῆσος, ἔτι μὴν καὶ τῷ
Οὐεργιουίῳ ὠκεανῷ. (*Periplus of the Outer Sea* 2 [prologue], 41–44)

The following are in the second book of Marcianus' periplus of
the Ocean east and west. . . .

Around the Prettanic Isles.

A periplus of the Prettanic Isle *Iwernia*.

A periplus of the Prettanic Isle *Albion*.

The Prettanic Isles:

The Prettanic Isles are two, one called *Albion* and the other
Iwernia. However, *Albion* is much larger. . . . *Iwernia*, the
other island, lies above this one, further to the west. It is
smaller in size and has the same placement as the previous
island. We will describe the periplus of this first, then
proceed to the larger island.

Periplus of the Prettanic Island *Iwernia*:

The Prettanic Island *Iwernia* is bordered on the north by the ocean
situated above and called *Hyperboreios*, on the east by the
ocean called *Iwernikos*, on the west by the western ocean, and
on the south by the ocean called *Wergiwios*. And the whole
arrangement of the island has this manner. . . .

The greatest length of the Prettanic Island of *Iwernia*, beginning at
the *Notion* Cape and ending at *Rhobogdion* Cape, so that the
length of the island is 3,170 stadia [634 kilometers]. The
width begins at the Sacred Cape and crosses over to
Rhobogdion Cape, so that the width of the island is 1,834

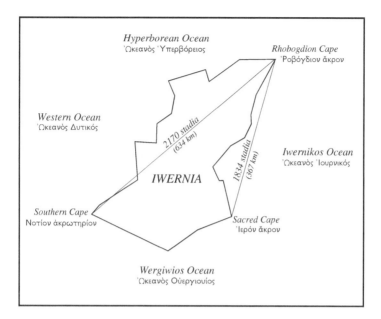

FIGURE 26. Ireland in Marcianus

stadia [367 kilometers]. Its capes are separated from the boundaries in this manner: the northern cape is distant from the Arctic Circle 14,250 stadia [2,850 kilometers]. The western cape . . . is 38,317 stadia [7,663 kilometers] from the equator. The eastern is 40,317 stadia [8,063 kilometers] from the east. It has 16 tribes, 11 noteworthy towns, 15 noteworthy rivers, 5 noteworthy capes, 6 noteworthy islands. The total circuit of *Iwernia* is not more than 9,085 stadia [1,817 kilometers], not less than 6,845 stadia [1,369 kilometers].

A Periplus of the Prettanic Island *Albion:*

The Prettanic island *Albion* is bounded . . . on the west by the *Iwernikos* Ocean, beyond which is *Iwernia*, and still further is the *Wergiwios* Ocean.

Marcianus takes the names and coordinates given in the text of Ptolemy and condenses them into a brief description of the seas and headlands of Ireland, along with some measurements of the dimensions and general position of the island on the world map (see Fig. 26). The summary of

Table 5. *Comparison of Geographical Features in Ptolemy and Marcianus*

Features in Ptolemy	Features in Marcianus
16 tribes	16 tribes
10 towns	11 noteworthy towns
15 rivers	15 noteworthy rivers
6 named capes	5 noteworthy capes
9 islands	6 noteworthy islands

tribes, towns, and physical features of Ireland is also based on Ptolemy's work, but the list does not correspond perfectly (see Table 5). The number of tribes in both authors is the same, as is the number of rivers, but Marcianus has one more town and one fewer cape than Ptolemy. This is easily explained if Marcianus, followed by some modern editors, took Ptolemy's *Isamnion* ('Ισάμνιον) on the east coast as a town instead of a cape.[198] But why Marcianus lists six noteworthy islands to Ptolemy's nine is more of a mystery. Ptolemy lists five *Aibudai* islands to the northeast of Ireland, *Monaoida* also to the northeast, and three other islands off the lower eastern coast, *Mona*, *Adru*, and *Limnu*.[199] The sixth-century lexicographer Stephanus of Byzantium relates that Marcianus elsewhere numbered five *Aibudai*, so perhaps here Marcianus is counting only *Monaoida* in addition to the *Aibudai* and not including the lower three.[200]

Stobaeus

Joannes Stobaeus composed an anthology of poets and prose-writers at the start of the fifth century A.D. that was originally intended for the education of his son. Although most of the work focuses on ethics, the first book is a collection of widely varied information, including geography and ethnography. It includes a brief ranking of the world's largest islands:

ἐν τούτῳ γε μὴν νῆσοι μεγάλαι τυγχάνουσιν, αἵ [τε] δύο Βρετανικαὶ λεγόμεναι [καὶ] Ἄλβιον καὶ Ἰέρνη, τῶν προϊστορημένων μείζους, ὑπὲρ Κελτοὺς κείμεναι. (*Anthologium* 1.40.1 [Wachsmuth 1884])

In this ocean are large islands, called the two Britannic Isles, *Albion* and *Iernē*, larger than those mentioned above, lying above the Celts.

This is almost a word-for-word rendition of the earlier passage from Pseudo-Aristotle's *De mundo*.[201]

Orosius

Orosius was a Christian writer and church official from Bracara Augusta (modern Braga) in northwest Spain who was an associate of both Augustine and Jerome. With Augustine's encouragement, he composed a seven-book *Histories against the Pagans* (*Historiae adversum paganos*), a world history from the creation until A.D. 417 that sought to defend the church against the charge that Christianity was bringing about the collapse of the Roman empire. Included in his first book is a survey of world geography, including a brief section on Ireland:

> *et quoniam oceanus habet insulas, quas Britanniam et Hiberniam vocant, quae in aversa Galliarum parte ad prospectum Hispaniae sitae sunt, breviter explicabuntur. . . . Hibernia insula inter Britanniam et Hispaniam sita longiore ab Africo in boream spatio porrigitur. huius partes priores intentae Cantabrico oceano Brigantiam Gallaeciae civitatem ab Africo sibi in circium occurrentem spatioso intervallo procul spectant, ab eo praecipue promunturio, ubi Scenae fluminis ostium est et Velabri Lucenique consistunt. haec propior Britanniae, spatio terrarum angustior, sed caeli solique temperie magis utilis, a Scottorum gentibus colitur. huic etiam Mevania insula proxima est et ipsa spatio non parva, solo commoda. aeque a Scottorum gentibus habitatur.* (*Historiae adversum paganos* 1.2.75, 80–82)

And since the ocean has islands which they call *Britannia* and *Hibernia*, which lie on the far side of Gaul looking toward *Hispania*, they shall be briefly described. . . . The island *Hibernia* lies between Britain and *Hispania*, with its greatest length extending from the southwest to the north. Its nearer parts stretching into the Cantabric Ocean look toward the city of *Brigantia* in *Gallaecia* from the southwest at a great distance, especially from the promontory where the mouth of the *Scena* is and the *Velabri* and *Luceni* dwell. This island is nearer to Britain, smaller in land area, but more advantageous in the temperateness of its climate and soil. It is inhabited by *Scotti*. Also near to this is the island of *Mevania*, itself not small, with favorable soil. The *Scotti* dwell on this island as well.

FIGURE 27. Orosius

Orosius returns to the traditional placement of Ireland between Britain and Spain, but does qualify the position by saying the island is nearer to Britain and at a great distance from *Brigantia* (modern La Coruña) in *Gallaecia*, the northwest corner of the Iberian peninsula (see Fig. 27). Although Orosius does not give any measurements, he notes that the greatest distance across Ireland is from the southwest to the north, an accurate assessment that follows Ptolemy and Marcianus.²⁰² He notes that Ireland is smaller than Britain, but, in the tradition of Pomponius Mela and Solinus, he says that its climate is excellent.²⁰³ Orosius also gives the name of one river, two tribes, and one island that have both similarities to and differences from those found in Ptolemy and other authors.²⁰⁴

The *Scena* River and the two tribes of the *Velabri* and *Luceni* are all placed in the southwestern part of the island, which faces Spain. It may only be coincidence, but Orosius focuses on the relationship between his homeland in northwest Spain and the southwest of Ireland. It is possible that he is drawing not only on earlier classical authors, but also on tales and traditions from his area of Spain, which may well have had an active trading relationship across the sea with Ireland. Orosius' *Scena* River is likely to be the modern Shannon (*Sinann* or *Sinna* in Old Irish), which Ptolemy, as the *Sēnu* (*Σήνου*), places in southwest Ireland. The *Velabri* tribe in Orosius are a certain match for Ptolemy's *Wellaboroi* (*Οὐελλάβοροι*), which the earlier geographer places in the southwestern corner of Ireland below his *Sēnu* River. But the *Luceni* tribe has no match in Ptolemy or in other ancient literature, though it is similar in name to the *Lucenses* tribe of northwestern Spain near *Brigantia* and Orosius' home of Bracara Augusta. Orosius is the first to clearly state that *Hibernia* is inhabited by the *Scotti*, as is the nearby island of *Mevania*, which is also agriculturally rich and large enough to merit special notice. *Mevania* is probably the Isle of Man.²⁰⁵ If so, it is worth noting that at least by Orosius' time, the *Scotti* had settled an island halfway across the Irish Sea to Britain, an excellent base for raids and settlements on their larger neighbor. That the Irish did settle on Man is shown by the Manx language, an offshoot of the Irish, not British, branch of the Celtic language family.

Pseudo-Agathemerus

Sometime after the second century A.D., an unknown author sometimes referred to as Pseudo-Agathemerus wrote a comparative geography of the world that included two brief references to Ireland. It is placed next to last in this study due to its uncertain date, but it may predate Solinus and many of the later authors:

νῆσοι δὲ ταύτης τῆς ἠπείρου ἀξιόλογοι ἐν μὲν τῇ ἐκτὸς θαλάσσῃ αἱ Βρετ-
τανικαὶ δύο Ἰουερνία τε καὶ Ἀλουίων. ἀλλ᾽ ἡ μὲν Ἰουερνία δυτικωτάτη

Table 6. *Ranking of Islands, by Size, among Ancient Authors*

Pseudo-Aristotle	*Ptolemy*	*Apuleius*	*Marcianus*	*Stobaeus*	*Pseudo-Agathemerus*
1. Britain	1. Sri Lanka	1. Britain	1. Sri Lanka	1. Britain	1. Sri Lanka
2. IRELAND	2. Britain	2. IRELAND	2. Britain	2. IRELAND	2. Britain
	3. Malay Peninsula		3. Malay peninsula		3. IRELAND
	4. IRELAND		4. IRELAND		

κειμένη, ἀντιπαρεκτείνεται μέχρι τινὸς τῇ Ἰσπανίᾳ· ἡ δὲ Ἀλουίων, ἐν ᾗ
καὶ τὰ στρατόπεδα ἵδρυται, μεγίστη τέ ἐστι καὶ ἐπιμηκεστάτη·

περὶ νήσων μεγίστων

τῶν δὲ νήσων τῶν πάνυ μεγίστων πρωτεύει μὲν παρὰ πάσας ἐν τῇ οἰκου-
μένῃ ἡ Σαλικὴ, δευτερεύει δὲ ἡ Ἀλουίων, τὰ δὲ τρίτα φέροιτ᾽ ἂν ἡ Ἰουερνία. (*Geographia compendaria* 4 [13], 8 [27] [*Geographi Graeci Minores*
2.497, 501])

Islands of the continent of Europe worthy of mention in the outer
sea are the two Brettanic Isles, *Iwernia* and *Albion. Iwernia* lies furthest to the west, extending some distance toward *Hispania. Albion,*
in which military camps are situated, is larger and very extensive. . . .

Concerning the Largest Islands

Of all the greatest islands among all those in the inhabited world,
Salike is first, second is *Albion,* and third would be *Iwernia.*

This passage is in the tradition that places Ireland between Britain and
Spain, but it does not specify how far the island extends toward the Iberian
peninsula. The second passage represents the final ranking in classical lit-
erature of Ireland among the major islands of the world (see Table 6).[206]
　Sri Lanka (*Salike*) vies with Britain for first place in size only in
Ptolemy, Marcianus, and Pseudo-Agathemerus. Elsewhere, Britain con-
sistently is in first place and always outranks Ireland.[207] The two tradi-
tions evident are those of Pseudo-Aristotle (of which both Apuleius and
Stobaeus are close translations) and Ptolemy (followed by Marcianus and
Pseudo-Agathemerus).

Stephanus of Byzantium

One final work with references to Ireland should be noted, even though
it is strictly of postclassical date. Stephanus of Byzantium, a grammarian
living in the sixth century A.D., composed the *Ethnica,* a sixty-book glossary of ethnic adjectives with added ethnographic lore. The remains of this
extensive work survive, however, only in an abridged *Epitome* made several
centuries after his death. Although Stephanus has little claim to originality,
his extensive use of earlier authors dating as far back as the sixth century

B.C. make him an important source for early ethnographic information. Three of his glossary items refer to Ireland:

Ἰέρνη, νῆσος ἐν τῷ πέρατι πρὸς δυσμαῖς. τὸ ἐθνικὸν Ἰερναῖος ὡς Λερναῖος.

Iernē, an island at the edge of the world toward the west. The ethnic name is *Iernaios*, like *Lernaios*.

Ἰουερνία, νῆσος Πρετανικὴ τῶν δύο ἐλάσσων. τὸ ἐθνικὸν Ἰουερνιάτης.

Iwernia, a Pretanic island, the lesser of the two. The ethnic name is *Iwerniatēs*.

Ἰουέρνη, πόλις ἐν τῷ Πρετανικῷ. τὸ ἐθνικὸν Ἰουέρνοι.

Iwernē, a Pretanic city. The ethnic name is *Iwernoi*.

Ptolemy (*Geography* 2.1) also lists an *Iwernoi* (Ἰουέρνοι) tribe and a town called *Iwernis* (Ἰουερνίς) in southern Ireland. Stephanus, as an insatiable collector of words, is drawing on Greek authors who both use and omit the *w* (ου) in *I(w)ernē* (Ἰ[ου]έρνη).

From Avienus to Stephanus of Byzantium, the literary sources on Ireland provide our clearest picture of relations between Ireland and the classical world. Although much of the information is incomplete, repetitive, and even fanciful, we are still able to construct a reasonably accurate picture of what the Greeks and Romans knew of this island at the edge of their world. Linguistics supports this literary evidence by strongly suggesting contacts between the Irish and outsiders, as shown through borrowings of both vocabulary and writing. Archaeology also contributes by providing physical evidence of trade contacts from at least the first century B.C. until the collapse of the western Roman empire—and undoubtedly there are many discoveries yet to be unearthed that will make the picture even clearer. But it is the literature that continues to serve as our primary source. For classical studies, these early writings on Ireland provide one of the best ethnographic examples of how the Greek and Roman world viewed the places and tribes beyond their lands. For students of Ireland, they are a vital source for the beginnings of Irish history.

NOTES

1. Avienus *Ora maritima* 108–19. Texts for *Ora maritima* include Berthelot 1934; Stichtenoth 1968; Murphy 1977.

2. *Odyssey* 5–8; Hesiod *Works and Days* 167–69. The phrase "holy island" occurs frequently in Greek literature, e.g., Hesiod *Theogony* 1015 (νήσων ἱεράων); Polybius 1.61.7 (τὴν Ἱερὰν νῆσον). Islands were also often sacred in Celtic tradition, from Posidonius' island of women worshiping Dionysus at the mouth of the river Loire (Strabo *Geography* 4.4.6) to the Arthurian isle of Avalon.

3. See O'Rahilly 1946a; Bergin 1946; Rivet and Smith 1979, 381–82; Koch 1991, 20–21. *Iweriu* became Old Irish *Ériu*, gen. *Érenn* ("Ireland").

4. Pomponius Mela *De chorographia* 3.53. Irish, along with all Celtic languages, lost the inherited sound *p*, so that Indo-European **piwer-* became Celtic **iwer-*. Homer uses a Greek cognate *píeira* (πίειρα), "fat, fertile, rich," an adjective applied often to land (e.g., *Iliad* 18.541; *Odyssey* 19.173). This root may also be present in the British river *Ivernium* (Rivet and Smith 1979, 381–82).

5. Herodotus 1.163, 4.152.

6. Hawkes 1977, 22–26. Hawkes still sees this *Ora maritima* passage as referring to Ireland and Britain, through Ephorus (c. 405–330 B.C.), from an early Massaliote source.

7. Pliny *Natural History* 2.169–70.

8. *Ora maritima* 380–89, 412–15. Avienus claims he is revealing information recorded by Himilco in the annals of the Carthaginians.

9. Strabo (3.5.11) relates that the Carthaginians had a monopoly on trade with Cassiterides, or "Tin Isles," of the Atlantic, though this trade may have been through intermediaries.

10. Pliny *Natural History* 4.102; Bede 1.1. *Albion* corresponds to Old Welsh *elbid*, Middle Welsh *elfyd*. See Koch 1991, 21; Rivet and Smith 1979, 247–48, 280–82.

11. Pliny *Natural History* 2.16.9.

12. He does provide some interesting information on other Celts, such as the fact that the young men of Gaul were punished for becoming fat (Strabo 4.4.6). Other references by Ephorus to the Celts are found in Strabo 1.2.28, 7.2.1 (see Freeman 1996, 34–37).

13. See Hawkes 1977.

14. Strabo *Geography* 2.4.1. Caesar (*Gallic War* 6.13) also gives the circumference of Britain, although he acknowledges that he only visited the southeast corner of the island.

15. Strabo *Geography* 2.5.8.

16. For example, Pseudo-Aristotle *De mundo* 3.393b.

17. Herodotus 3.115. Strabo *Geography* 2.5.8: ὁ μὲν οὖν Μασσαλιώτης Πυθέας τὰ περὶ Θούλην τὴν βορειοτάτην τῶν Βρεττανίδων ὕστατα λέγει (Pytheas of Massalia says that Thule, the northernmost of the Bretannic Isles, is the most distant.)

18. Timaeas, via Pliny, says that tin was brought from the island of Mictis, six days' voyage from Britain, by Britons in wicker and leather boats (Pliny *Natural History* 4.16). Diodorus Siculus calls the island *Ictis* (5.22).

19. For example, the Celts' dress and customs (2.17), their bravery in battle (2.28), and the fortitude of Celtic women (21.38).

20. Polybius 34.10 (see Strabo 4.2.1).

21. Polybius 3.57.

22. The fragments of Posidonius on the Celts are preserved in Athenaeus 4.151–54, 6.246; Diodorus Siculus 5.25–32; Strabo 2.5.28, 4.1–4. The debt of Caesar to Posidonius (*Gallic War* 6.11–28) is debatable. See Tierney 1960; Nash 1976.

23. Strabo 3.2.9.

24. Ptolemy *Almagest* 2.6.25–27.

25. Strabo 4.5.4; Jerome *Adversus Jovinianum* 2.7. Geoffrey Keating, the famed seventeenth-century Irish historian, denies (*History of Ireland*, Intro. 2) the charges of cannibalism and other vices laid on the Irish by ancient authors such as Strabo (2.5.8, 4.5.4), Pomponius Mela (*De chorographia* 3.53), Solinus (*Collectanea rerum memorabilium* 22.2–6), and Jerome (*Adversus Jovinianum* 2.7, *Epistle* 69.415). He cites as the only exception to cannibalism the tale of Eithne, daughter of an ancient king of Leinster, who was supposedly reared on the flesh of children.

26. Diodorus Siculus (17.10.2) uses the same word when he refers to a rainbow. *Iris* also would have been known to Diodorus as a river in Asia Minor.

27. Iris does have some coincidental association with the north and west, as it was she who summoned Boreas (the north wind) and Zephyrus (the west wind) to aid Achilles in the *Iliad* (23.192–216).

28. Homer *Odyssey* 10.116–24; Herodotus 1.216, 3.38, 4.26. Aristotle (*Nichomachean Ethics* 7.5) echoes Herodotus' description, saying that a tribe near the Black Sea delights in human flesh.

29. Pliny *Natural History* 30.13.

30. See Allen 1978, 43–45.

31. Strabo *Geography* 1.4.4; 2.1.13, 17.

32. Caesar *Gallic War* 3.8. Caesar states (*Gallic War* 4.20) that he gathered together Gaulish merchants prior to his first invasion of Britain in 55 B.C. to collect information on the island. The Gauls reportedly were familiar only with the British coast opposite Gaul and knew nothing of the size or ethnography of the island—a difficult statement to entirely believe if Britain, as Caesar says, was a constant source of help to the Gauls in their war against Rome (4.20) as well as a training center for Gaulish druids (6.13).

33. Caesar here probably uses the name *Mona* for the Isle of Man, as does Ptolemy (*Geography* 2.1), since both place the island far off the British coast. However, Tacitus (*Agricola* 14, 18) clearly uses the same name to mean the island of Anglesey (Welsh *Môn*), just off the Welsh coast, and Pliny (*Natural History* 2.187, 4.103) also seems to identify *Mona* with Anglesey rather than Man.

34. Pliny *Natural History* 4.102–3; Tacitus *Agricola* 24.

35. Ptolemy *Geography* 2. See Tierney 1959.

36. In his survey of classical sources for Ireland, Kenney (1929, 130) includes a line written by the Roman poet Propertius c. 16 B.C. in the generation between Caesar and Strabo: *hibernique Getae, pictoque Britannia curru* ("the wintry Getae, Britain with its painted chariots," 4.3.9). The inclusion of this passage by Kenney

is an error based on the mistaken translation of *hiberni* as "the Irish" rather than as the nominative-plural adjective of *hibernus* ("wintry, northern") modifying *Getae* (a masculine noun in spite of the *-ae* ending), a Thracian tribe on the Danube.

37. Strabo *Geography* 4.5.3.

38. The description of the late-fourth-century B.C. voyage of Pytheas from Massalia on the Mediterranean coast of Gaul to Britain, Thule, and the lands of northwest Europe survives only in scattered fragments quoted by later authors.

39. Strabo *Geography* 1.4.2, 2.4.1, 2.5.8.

40. Ptolemy identifies Mainland, the largest of the Shetlands, as Thule (*Geography* 2.2); Tacitus only says that Agricola's fleet saw Thule while sailing by the Shetlands.

41. Few Mediterranean imports from Strabo's time or earlier survive in the archaeological record to indicate commercial contact, though both Tacitus (*Agricola* 24) and Ptolemy (*Geography* 1.11) specifically mention merchants sailing to Ireland toward the end of the first century A.D.

42. As a unit of linear measurement, the Greek stade (στάδιον) contained 600 feet, though the length of the foot depended on the particular standard (Olympic, Pergamene, etc.). In this book I use a ratio of 1 stade = 200 meters throughout, but the exact length intended by a particular author is often debatable.

43. Strabo *Geography* 1.4.3–4.

44. Several decades before Strabo, Diodorus Siculus (5.21–22) believed that even Britain was very cold, though Caesar (*Gallic War* 5.12) notes soon after Diodorus that the climate of Britain is milder than that of Gaul. Roughly twenty years after Strabo, Pomponius Mela (*De chorographia* 3.53) says that Ireland's climate is relatively mild. At the end of the century, Tacitus (*Agricola* 24) relates that Ireland's climate differs little from that of Britain. Marcianus (*Periplus of the Outer Sea* 2.41) writes in the early fifth century A.D. that Ireland lies above Britain and to the west, but he may just be referring to the fact that Ireland is slightly farther north in latitude than southern Britain, as shown in Ptolemy's *Geography*, his primary source.

45. Strabo *Geography* 2.5.7. Interestingly, he does not rule out the possible existence of other unknown inhabitable areas of land within this northern temperate zone (*Geography* 1.4.6, 2.5.13).

46. See also Strabo *Geography* 2.1.4–5, 17; 15.1.12; Pliny *Natural History* 6.58.

47. An astronomical cubit equals two degrees.

48. Herodotus 2.30; Strabo *Geography* 16.4.8, 17.1.2.

49. Caesar *Gallic War* 5.13.

50. Strabo's key clause, πρόμηκες μᾶλλον πλάτος ἔχουσα, very literally translates as "having elongation (πρόμηκες) more than breadth (πλάτος)." In his earlier passage (*Geography* 2.5.14), Strabo clearly says that the πλάτος (*platos*) of the inhabitable world stretches north-south through the Nile from the parallel of Ireland to the parallel running through Africa. Thus it seems reasonable to take the smaller dimension (*platos*) in this passage as north-south as well. See Tierney 1959, 140–41.

51. Diodorus Siculus 5.32.3. Jerome also accuses the *Atticoti* or *Scoti* of cannibalism (*Adversus Jovinianum* 2.7).

52. Herodotus 1.216, 3.38, 4.26.

53. Later in the same century, Pliny ascribes cannibalism to many barbarian tribes, especially those such as the Arimaspi in the far north of the world (*Natural History* 7.9–12), though he does not claim the Irish eat human flesh.

54. He mentions the Celts (Caesar *Gallic War* 7.77) and Iberians (Valarius Maximus 7.6), but conveniently forgets to mention that even Greeks were known to practice cannibalism in extreme situations (Thucydides *Peloponnesian War* 2.70).

55. Caesar *Gallic War* 5.14; Herodotus 1.216; 3.101; 4.104, 172, 180. As noted earlier, Ephorus wrote that gluttony was punished among the Gauls (Strabo *Geography* 4.4.6).

56. "We are charged with three crimes: atheism, Thyestean feasts, and Oedipodean intercourse" (Athenagoras *Legatio* 3).

57. Caesar *Gallic War* 5.13. Pliny relates that both Pytheas and Isidorus give the circumference of Britain as a slightly smaller 4,875 Roman miles (7,215 kilometers) (*Natural History* 4.102).

58. In an earlier passage (2.78), Pomponius briefly refers to a battle of Hercules with Albion and Bergyon (or Dercynon in some manuscripts) that may be a garbled reference to Ireland (see Rhys 1882, 200–203): *alioqui litus ignobile est, Lapideum ut vocant, in quo Herculem contra Albiona et Bergyon. Neptuni liberos dimicantem cum tela defecissent ab invocato Jove adiutum imbre lapidum ferunt. credas pluvisse, adeo multi passim et late iacent.* (In general the shore called Lapideum ["stony"], where Hercules fought Albion and Bergyon, is unknown. They say that when fighting these sons of Neptune, his spears failed, but he called on Jupiter, who rained down a shower of stones. Believe as you will concerning the shower, but many stones are scattered there far and wide.)

In his tenth labor, Hercules travels to the far west, slays the three-headed monster Geryon, and claims his cattle. His return voyage through Spain, Gaul, and Italy is constantly hampered by local tribes, as well as by these two giants in Liguria on the Mediterranean coast near Massalia. Albion certainly can be a name for Britain, but to derive Bergyon from any of the common terms for Ireland requires both skill and imagination. It is intriguing, however, that Albion and Bergyon are "sons of Neptune," which could be a poetic metaphor for islands in the sea.

59. Caesar *Gallic War* 5.13; Isidorus *Geographi Graeci Minores* 2.509.

60. Strabo *Geography* 4.5.4. The fact that Mela says Ireland is roughly the same size as Britain is no help, as he does not give dimensions for Britain either, though he says it is triangular in shape, like Sicily (3.50).

61. The name *Iuverna* is clearly distinct from the * Iernē* (Ἰέρνη) of Strabo and Isidorus, though close to the *Iwernia* (Ἰουερνία) of Ptolemy. Latin does not regularly allow a sequence of *i* + *v* (pronounced as English *w*) followed by a vowel without inserting a *u* between the *i* and the *v*. Therefore the Greek root *Iwern-* would become *Iuvern-* in Latin.

62. Justin *Epitome* 44.4.14.

63. Curtius *History* 5.1.12. Solinus (*Collectanea rerum memorabilium* 22.2–6) repeats Mela's claim concerning Irish cattle.

64. Strabo *Geography* 4.5.4; Diodorus Siculus 5.32.3. The Latin term *pietas*

should not be simply read as "piety," in spite of the obvious etymological connection. Rather, it is a sense of dutiful respect and conduct not only toward the gods but toward family and country as well.

65. Pomponius Mela *De chorographia* 3.51.

66. Pliny *Natural History* Preface 17.

67. Pliny *Natural History* 1 (Table of Contents for Book Four).

68. Ptolemy *Geography* 1.11. Pliny does directly cite Philemon as a source in his discussion of the North Sea and Baltic regions (*Natural History* 4.95; 37.33, 36). This is assuming that Pliny and Ptolemy are referring to the same Philemon, who bears a common Greek name.

69. Ireland is in fact almost 500 kilometers (c. 340 Roman miles) from southwest to northeast and roughly 300 kilometers (c. 200 Roman miles) east to west.

70. Strabo *Geography* 4.5.4.

71. For example, the *latitudo* of the inhabitable world is north-south (2.245); the *longitudo* of Further Spain is east-west (3.6); and the *latitudo* of southern Gaul is north-south and its *longitudo* east-west (3.37). The east-west spread of the Alps from the Adriatic to the Mediterranean is *longitudo*, whereas the *latitudo* is north-south (3.132), as it is in Crete (4.58) and the Red Sea (6.163).

72. They are first mentioned by Pomponius Mela (*De chorographia* 2.6, 3.54), who says there are only thirty.

73. Mela also has seven *Haemodae* (3.54) facing Germany, which are almost certainly the same as Pliny's *Acmodae*. The Shetlands were identified as the land of Thule by Agricola's fleet according to Tacitus (*Agricola* 10) and Ptolemy (*Geography* 2.2).

74. Pliny is the first to mention these islands, which in Ptolemy appear as the *Aibudai* (Αἰβοῦδαι) (*Geography* 2.1) and *Ebudai* (Ἔβουδαι) (*Almagest* 2.6.28).

75. Caesar *Gallic War* 5.13.

76. Ptolemy *Geography* 2.1.

77. Tacitus *Agricola* 14, 18; *Annals* 14.29.

78. Ptolemy *Geography* 2.1; Orosius 1.2.82. Bede (*Historia ecclesiastica* 2.5) apparently groups Man and Anglesey together as the plural *Menavae*. See Rivet and Smith 1979, 410–11.

79. Ptolemy *Geography* 2.1.

80. *Vectis* may be the same as *Iktis* (Ἴκτις) in Diodorus Siculus (5.22). Suetonius (8.4.1), who wrote in the early second century A.D., also has *Vectis*, and Ptolemy (*Geography* 2.2) calls the island *Wēktis* (Οὐηκτίς) as well.

81. *Silumnus* may be the same as the *Siluram insulam* in Solinus (22.7). Ptolemy (*Geography* 2.1) places the island of *Adru* (Ἄδρου) just off the coast of east-central Ireland.

82. Caesar *Gallic War* 5.13.

83. Strabo *Geography* 1.4.3, 4.5.4.

84. Pomponius Mela *De chorographia* 3.54.

85. Tacitus *Agricola* 24; Ptolemy *Geography* 1.11.

86. Isidorus in *Geographi Graeci Minores* 2.509. Britain and Ireland are in-

deed larger than any of the Mediterranean islands: Britain is 230,000 sq. km; Ireland 82,460 sq. km; Sicily 25,462 sq. km; Crete 8,380 sq. km.

87. Strabo *Geography* 2.5.8.

88. As seen previously in Caesar (*Gallic War* 5.13). See also Tacitus *Agricola* 10.

89. Pseudo-Aristotle *De mundo* 3.393b. Tacitus (*Agricola* 10) breaks with the tradition that Britain is triangular and follows the Roman historians Livy and Fabius Rusticus in saying that it is elongated and shaped like a double-edged ax (*bipennis*).

90. Caesar *Gallic War* 5.13.

91. Tacitus *Agricola* 12. This is a marked difference from Strabo (*Geography* 1.4.4, 2.5.8), writing earlier in the same century, who describes Ireland as a barely habitable wasteland. Tacitus is in accord with the more generous and accurate descriptions of Pomponius Mela (*De chorographia* 3.53).

92. Tacitus *Agricola* 11–12.

93. See Mac Cana 1985.

94. Tacitus *Agricola* 11. Caesar (*Gallic War* 5.12, 14) also notes the similarities between the Gauls and inhabitants of southern Britain.

95. Caesar uses almost the same words (*Gallic War* 4.20) in describing his first invasion of Britain in 54 B.C., claiming that the invasion was intended as a large-scale reconnaissance of the "localities, ports, and approaches" (*loca, portus, aditus cognovisset*).

96. The phrase *in melius* ("better, for the better") appears in the oldest manuscripts, but it is very difficult to make this clause work properly if one accepts this reading. Tacitus uses *in melius* eight times in his surviving writings aside from this passage, though never at the beginning of a clause (a very rare usage in any Latin writer). See Ogilvie and Richmond 1967, 237.

97. See Ptolemy *Geography* 1.11.

98. *marggad mór na nGall ngrécach* (Gwynn 1913, 24–25). In its earliest attestations, the Old Irish noun *Gall* means "a Gaul" from the area of modern-day France, but later it is used more generally as "foreigner."

99. The other possibility is Jerome's nemesis Pelagius, who was reportedly of *Scotti* lineage (Jerome *Commentary on Jeremiah* 3, prologue). The term *regulus* is the diminutive of the Latin *rex* ("king") and is commonly used either for the leader of a small group or for a king's son, though Livy (5.38.3) calls Brennus, whose sizable army sacked Rome in 390 B.C., a *regulus Gallorum* ("chieftain of the Gauls").

100. For example, Suetonius states that a British ruler fled to Caligula (Suetonius *Caligula* 44).

101. For example, Ogilvie and Richmond 1967, 238; Warner 1995. The setting of *seditio domestica* ("internal discord") for the exile of Agricola's Irish king suggests contention within a family, perhaps over succession. But this is not especially helpful in pinning down a particular person, as there were dozens of *tuatha*, or small tribal kingdoms, in ancient Ireland, and rarely, according to Irish literature, did power pass smoothly within them.

102. The less-experienced Strabo (*Geography* 4.5.3) makes an almost identical claim concerning Britain before the Claudian conquest.

103. A brief survey of the invasion hypothesis is found in Killeen 1976, 213–15.

104. The *Historia Augusta* similarly uses Ireland as a clearly rhetorical device to indicate the "end of the earth" in the early fourth century A.D. (Tacitus *Historia Augusta* 15.2).

105. Silius *Italicus Punica* 17.239.

106. Agricola's army conquered the Orkney Islands in A.D. 84 (Tacitus *Agricola* 10) and subjugated the area of northern Britain "famed for its short nights" (*Agricola* 12) during this and the previous four years (*Agricola* 22–38).

107. Pseudo-Aristotle *De mundo* 3.393b.

108. The properties of each latitude or parallel in the northern hemisphere are discussed in the whole of *Almagest* 2.6.

109. Pseudo-Aristotle *De mundo* 3.393b.

110. Strabo *Geography* 1.4.4–5; 2.1.13, 17–18; 2.5.8, 14, 34.

111. Ptolemy *Geography* 1.6. Editions include Nobbe 1843 (Books 4–8) and Müller 1883 (Books 1–3). I have followed the numbering system of E. Stevenson 1932, the standard English translation.

112. Ptolemy *Geography* 1.7–11.

113. Pliny *Natural History* 1 (Table of Contents).

114. Tacitus *Agricola* 24.

115. Ptolemy *Almagest* 2.6.25–27.

116. One exception is the island of Taprobane (Sri Lanka), where he describes the country as rich in rice, jewels, metals, elephants, and tigers, and the women as covered with hair (*Geography* 7.4).

117. Taking one degree of latitude in Ptolemy as approximately 500 stadia (Rivet and Smith 1979, 107) or 100 kilometers, Ireland would be roughly 450 kilometers north to south in the *Geography*, compared to Pliny's (*Natural History* 4.102–3) 444 kilometers and the almost 500 kilometers on modern maps. On the position of Ireland before Ptolemy, see Caesar (*Gallic War* 5.13), Pliny (*Natural History* 4.102–3), and Tacitus (*Agricola* 24). Ireland is, however, about 2 degrees too far north relative to Britain in Ptolemy.

118. Some examples of this approach are Orpen 1894; O'Rahilly 1946b, 1–42; Pokorny 1953. Though I make use of the identifications given by these scholars, especially O'Rahilly, most are my own based on careful comparison of Ptolemy's text with medieval names and features on modern maps of Ireland.

119. Ptolemy's Greek numeration system uses accented letters instead of separate numeral signs (e.g., α'=1, β'=2, γ'=3, ι'=10, κ'=20), with ʟ″ a special sign for half and all fractions represented by a double accent (e.g., γ'' = 1/3, or 20 minutes, of arch).

120. The only other writer to use the term is the late classical geographer Marcianus (*Periplus of the Outer Sea* 2.42), who frequently repeats Ptolemy while adding little new information.

121. Ptolemy *Geography* 7.4.

122. Ptolemy's text reads, "the mouth of the *Rhawiu* River" ('Ραουίου ποτα-μοῦ ἐκβολαί), where 'Ραουίου could be the Greek genitive singular of an *o*-stem

Rhawios (*Ῥαουίος) or simply the nominative case of a native word ending in -*u* (Ῥαουίου). Since Ptolemy uses the same formula for river names ending in -*a* (for example, Αὐσόβα ποταμοῦ ἐκβολαί) and does not use a feminine genitive-singular ending in these cases, it seems reasonable to take these names ending in -*u* as nominative as well, though this is not certain.

123. Some manuscripts have *Nagnata* (Νάγνατα) for the town and *Nagnatai* (Ναγνᾶται) for the tribe. The epithet *episēmos* (ἐπίσημος) with *Magnata* town is a Greek word meaning "designated" or "distinguished" and seems to be a later addition to the manuscript.

124. Ptolemy (*Geography* 8.3) himself notes that the town of *Iwernis* has the same basic name as Ireland (*Iwernia*). A similar river name in Britain is the *Ibernio*, perhaps representing *Iwernion* (Rivet and Smith 1979, 381–82). Herodian (*De prosodia catholica* 12.327) says there is a city named *Iwernē* (Ἰουέρνη) in the Pretannic Sea.

125. Orosius *Historiae adversum paganos* 1.2.80–82.

126. Marcianus *Periplus of the Outer Sea* 2.42, 44.

127. Regardless of the original beginning of the word, the termination -*ona* is common in Celtic divine names, most notably rivers named for goddesses (e.g., *Matrona* "sacred mother" > Marne River of France). Also compare the Severn (Welsh *Hafren*) River of southeastern Wales, listed as *Sabrina* in Ptolemy (*Geography* 2.2).

128. A characteristic Roman burial was unearthed upriver from Waterford Harbor along the River Nore, a tributary of the Barrow.

129. Avienus *Ora maritima* 108–19; Ptolemy *Geography* 2.4. These names may be related to the sailors' practice of building shrines or even temples on prominent headlands.

130. Some of the many examples include the place name *Brigantia* on the Iberian peninsula (Orosius 1.2.71) and *Brigantium* in the Alps (Strabo *Geography* 4.1.3).

131. Pliny *Natural History* 4.103.

132. The name probably derives from *Bou-vinda*, "white cow." Compare the island off the west coast of Ireland in Bede *Historia Ecclesiastica* 4.4: "In the secret language of the Irish called *Boufinde*, the island of the white calf" (*secreta sermone Scottico Inis boufinde, id est insula vitulae albae, nuncupatur*).

133. Stephanus of Byzantium (*Epitome:* Σάμνιον) lists a similar *Samnion* as a "Pretanic" town (Σάμνιον, πόλις Πρετανίας). Marcianus (*Periplus of the Outer Sea* 2.43) seems to count *Isamnion* as a cape instead of a town.

134. The *Logia* matches the River Lagan both in position and in name, with Irish *Loíg* being the genitive of Old Irish *loég* ("calf")—in *Logia*, specifically a female calf.

135. See Ptolemy *Geography* 2.10.

136. Ptolemy *Geography* 2.2, 6–7.

137. Ptolemy *Almagest* 2.6; Pliny *Natural History* 4.103.

138. Pliny *Natural History* 4.103.

139. Adamnan's *Life of St. Columba* (1.22, 41; 2.22) has *Malea*, whereas the Gaelic name is *Muile*.

140. Ptolemy *Geography* 2.2.

141. See the discussion under Pliny *Natural History* 4.103.

142. Pliny *Natural History* 4.103. *Adru* may be the peninsula of Howth (Irish *Étar*) in Dublin Bay, while *Limnu* may be Lambay Island just to its north.

143. See Ptolemy *Almagest* 2.6.25–27.

144. See Pseudo-Aristotle *De mundo* 3.393b.

145. Some parts of Herodian's text have been partially reconstructed from later works by the modern editor and may therefore be suspect.

146. Ptolemy *Geography* 2.1.

147. Ibid.

148. Two passages (on Irish mothers feeding their infants with the tip of a sword and the Irish use of leather boats) commonly assigned to this section of Solinus are almost certainly later additions and are not included in standard editions.

149. Pomponius Mela *De chorographia* 3.53.

150. Solinus *Collectanea rerum memorabilium* 22.8. The seventh-century writer Isidorus (*Etymologiae* 14.6.2–6) echoes Solinus' statement on the snakes of Thanet. Although there are no true snakes in Ireland, a few specimens of the European Slow Worm (*Anguis fragilis*) have been found in the Burren area of County Clare in western Ireland. This legless lizard can easily be mistaken for a small snake, but the first definite record of its existence in Ireland dates only from 1977. Whether it is a native Irish species or a recent import is unknown. That bees were well established at least in medieval Ireland is shown by the extensive Irish laws on beekeeping found in the *Bechbretha* (Charles-Edwards and Kelly 1983). The medieval writer Giraldus Cambrensis (*Topographia Hiberniae* 2) notes Solinus' mistake, but he concedes that it is possible bees were introduced to Ireland after the time of Solinus.

151. Pliny *Natural History* 3.78–79.

152. Interestingly, the Irish had an inherited Indo-European word for snake, *nathir*, related to Latin *natrix* ("water-snake").

153. Pomponius Mela *De chorographia* 3.53.

154. Pliny *Natural History* 4.102–3.

155. The absence of third-century literary references to Ireland is closely matched by a noticeable gap in Roman archaeological remains from this time recovered in Ireland.

156. Literary evidence for invasion of and raids on Britain during these centuries, aside from this panegyric, includes Pactatus *Panegyric on Theodosius* 5.2; Ammianus Marcellinus 26.4.5, 27.8; and Claudian *Panegyric on the Third Consulship of Honorius* 54–56, *Panegyric on the Fourth Consulship of Honorius* 8.30–33, *On the Consulship of Stilicho* 2.247–55, *Gothic War* 416–18.

157. A few years later, the anonymous author of the *Panegyric on Constantine Augustus* (7.2) includes the Caledonians, a group defeated by Agricola in the first century A.D., among the Picts. Ammianus Marcellinus (*History* 27.8.5) divides them into the *Dicalydones* and the *Verturiones*. At least some of the Pictish tribes may have been Celtic in origin and speech, but Celts were related more closely in language to the Britons and the Gauls than to the Irish (see K. Jackson 1954).

158. Beginning with *Nomina provinciarum omnium* 13 in c. A.D. 312.

159. Pomponius Mela *De chorographia* 2.6; Ptolemy *Geography* 2.2; Orosius *Historiae adversum paganos* 1.2.75–82. Pliny (*Natural History* 4.102–3) gives the number as forty.

160. Tacitus *Agricola* 23; Ptolemy *Geography* 2.2.

161. For example, *in Ionio mari*, "in the Ionian Sea" (*Maritime Itinerary* 523.4).

162. As there are many textual problems with this passage, it is best not to try to read too much into this unusual form. St. Patrick in his fifth-century *Confession* (1, 16, etc.) uses the very similar term *Hiberione*.

163. See the previous *Panegyric on Constantius Caesar* 11.4.

164. Thule was a northern land first described by Pytheas that may have originally referred to Iceland or one of the island groups off northern Britain, but in common Greek and Roman usage had become a proverbial expression for the ends of the earth. The Isles of the Blessed (*fortunatae insulae*) were a mythical land of the privileged dead (see Hesiod *Works and Days* 171), later identified by geographers with the Canary Islands off the western coast of Africa. Here they are used in their original mythological sense.

165. See Tacitus *Agricola* 24.

166. *Panegyric on Constantius Caesar* 11.4.

167. *Ibid.*

168. *Panegyric on Constantine Augustus* 7.2.

169. Other instances of Picts and *Scot(t)i* grouped together are Ammianus Marcellinus *History* 20.1.1, 26.4.5, 27.8.5; Claudian *Panegyric on the Third Consulship of the Emperor Honorius* 54–56, *Panegyric on the Fourth Consulship of the Emperor Honorius* 8.30–33, *On Stilicho's Consulship* 2.247–55, *Gothic War* 416–18.

170. Jerome *Commentary on Jeremiah* 3, (prologue); Claudian *Panegyric on the Fourth Consulship of the Emperor Honorius* 8.30–33.

171. Claudian *On Stilicho's Consulship* 2.247–55.

172. Prosper Tiro *Chronicle* 431. Isidorus (*Etymologiae* 14.6.6) states: "*Scotia*, which is the same as *Hibernia* very near the isle of Britain . . . from [the name of the Hibernian ocean] is the name *Hibernia*. However, it is called *Scotia* because the *Scotti* dwell there." (*Scotia, idem et Hibernia proxima Brittaniae insula . . . unde et Hibernia dicta. Scotia autem, quod ab Scotorum gentibus colitur, appellata.*)

173. Evans 1967, 374. One example is the name *Scota* from the first- and second-century A.D. pottery works at La Graufesenque.

174. See Vian 1987.

175. Text in Mynors 1964, 85. This "barbarian conspiracy" of the Saxons, Picts, and *Scoti* is also discussed by Ammianus Marcellinus (*History* 27.8.5).

176. Ammianus Marcellinus *History* 27.8. Substantial hoards of Roman material from the fourth and early fifth centuries, possibly collected in such raids, have been unearthed in Ireland. See also Claudian *Panegyric on the Third Consulship of Honorius* 51–56, *Panegyric on the Fourth Consulship of Honorius* 24–33.

177. Ptolemy *Geography* 2.1; Claudian *Panegyric on the Third Consulship of Honorius* 54–56.

178. Ammianus groups together Picts, Saxons, *Scotti*, and *Attacotti* in his sec-

ond passage, and Picts, *Attacotti*, and *Scotti* in his third, but Jerome pairs the *Scotti* and *Atticoti* alone (*Epistle ad Oceanum* 69.415).

179. Jerome *Adversus Jovinianum* 2.7. Jerome calls the *Atticoti* or *Scoti* (depending on the manuscript) a "British people" (*gentem Britannicam*).

180. *Notitia dignitatum* East 9.8; West 5.48, 51, 70, 197, 200, 218; 7.24, 74, 78. It is tempting to see the name *Atecotti* and its variants deriving from the Celtic intensive or pejorative prefix *ate-* (Evans 1967, 142–45) combined with the name *Scotti* (**Ate-scotti > Ate-cotti*), with the loss of the -s- in euphonic combination, to designate a separate and particularly unpleasant tribal group.

181. See Pacatus *Panegyric on Theodosius* 5.2; Ammianus Marcellinus *History* 28.3; Claudian *Panegyric on the Third Consulship of Honorius* 54–56, *Panegyric on the Fourth Consulship of Honorius* 8.30–33.

182. Jerome *Adversus Jovinianum* 2.7.

183. See *Historia Augusta—Probus* 24.1–3.

184. Ammianus Marcellinus *History* 27.8.5.

185. An echo of such expeditions may be present in the Old Irish dynastic poetry of Leinster, in which the pre-Christian king Núadu Necht is said to have "fettered Gaulish hostages as far as the five peaks of the Alps" (Koch and Carey 1995, 45).

186. *Notitia dignitatum* East 9.8; West 5.48, 51, 70, 197, 200, 218; 7.24, 74, 78.

187. The charge of cannibalism among the Irish is found earlier in Diodorus Siculus 5.32.3 and Strabo *Geography* 4.5.4.

188. Pomponius Mela *De chorographia* 3.53; Solinus *Collectanea rerum memorabilium* 22.2–6.

189. Caesar *Gallic War* 5.14.

190. Strabo *Geography* 4.5.2.

191. Grattius (*Cynegeticon* 174–81); Oppian (*Cynegetica* 1.468–80); Nemesianus (*Cynegetica* 225); Claudian (*On the Consulship of Stilicho* 3.301). That dogs were a commodity exported from Ireland is suggested by St. Patrick himself, who relates in his autobiography that he escaped slavery in Ireland on a ship containing many dogs (*Confession* 19).

192. Strabo *Geography* 1.4.4.

193. Ammianus Marcellinus *History* 27.8.5; Pacatus *Panegyric on Theodosius* 5.2. But note that neither Claudian nor Pacatus mentions the *Attacotti*.

194. Orosius *Historiae adversum paganos* 1.2.80–82. The term *Hiverne* seems to be a combination of Greek *Iernē* (᾽Ιέρνη) and Latin *Hibernia*, appropriate for a native Greek-speaker turned Latin poet.

195. See Strabo *Geography* 1.4.4, 2.1.13, 2.5.8.

196. Text in Müller 1855, vol. 1. See Pseudo-Aristotle *De mundo* 3.393b; Dionysius Periegetes *Orbis descriptio* 565–69; Ptolemy *Geography* 7.5; Apuleius *De mundo* 7.

197. The distance from the westernmost promontory of Ireland to the western end of the world is missing from the manuscript.

198. Ptolemy *Geography* 2.1.

199. Ibid.

200. Stephanus of Byzantium *Ethnica Epitome:* "*Aibudai:* five Pretannic Islands, according to Marcianus in his *Periplus*" (Ἀιβοῦδαι, νῆσοι πέντε τῆς Πρεταννικῆς, ὡς Μαρκιανὸς ἐν περίπλῳ).

201. Pseudo-Aristotle *De mundo* 3.393b. See also Apuleius *De mundo* 7.

202. Ptolemy *Geography* 2.1; Marcianus *Periplus of the Outer Sea* 2.43.

203. Pomponius Mela *De chorographia* 3.53; Solinus *Collectanea rerum memorabilium* 22.2–6.

204. Ptolemy *Geography* 2.1.

205. Orosius is the first to use the name *Mevania*. He is followed by Julius Honorius (*Cosmographia* 16–17), probably in the fifth century, and Jordanes (*Getica* 1.8) in the mid-sixth century. Bede (*Historia ecclesiastica* 2.9) in the early eighth century refers to both Man and Anglesey together as the *Mevaniae*. Pliny (*Natural History* 4.103) probably intends the Isle of Man by his *Monapia*.

206. Pseudo-Aristotle *De mundo* 3.393b; Ptolemy *Geography* 7.5; Apuleius *De mundo* 7; Marcianus *Periplus of the Outer Sea* 1.8. This list does not include the authors who simply compare the size of Ireland to Britain. Dionysius Periegetes (*Orbis descriptio* 565–69) does not specifically name Britain and Ireland, but says the two *Bretanides* islands are the largest in the world.

207. The only exception to this is in Isidorus (*Geographi Graeci Minores* 2.509), but this is probably a textual error.

The Greek Alphabet

Uppercase Greek	Lowercase Greek	English equivalent	Sound
A	α	a	*fa*ther
B	β	b	*b*iology
Γ	γ	g	hard *g*, as in *g*ood
Δ	δ	d	*d*ental
E	ε	e	short *e*, as in p*e*pper
Z	ζ	z	*zd*, as in glaz*ed*
H	η	ē	long *a*, as in l*a*bor
Θ	θ	th	*th*in
I	ι	i	when short, like the *i* in *i*nsular, when long, like the *i* in pol*i*ce
K	κ	k	*k*eep
Λ	λ	l	*l*iberate
M	μ	m	*m*odern
N	ν	n	*n*ext
Ξ	ξ	x	*ks*, as in ta*x*i
O	ο	o	short *o*, as in *o*pera
Π	π	p	*p*aternal
P	ρ	r	aspirated *r*, as in *rh*inoceros
Σ	σ/ς	s	*s*imple
T	τ	t	*t*able

Uppercase Greek	Lowercase Greek	English equivalent	Sound
Υ	υ	y	fronted *u*, when short, like French t*u*, when long, like German *ü*ber
Φ	φ	ph	*Ph*iladelphia
Χ	χ	ch	as in German i*ch* or Scottish lo*ch*
Ψ	ψ	ps	as in ecli*ps*e
Ω	ω	ō	long *o*, as in *o*de
Ου	ου	w, u	*w*agon (as a consonant); m*oo*n (as a diphthong)
‛		h	(aspirated)
’		—	(unaspirated)
;		?	(question mark)

Classical References to Ireland

Author	Passage(s)	Date	Summary
Sources for Avienus' *Ora maritima*	*Ora maritima* 108–19	c. 500 B.C.	Sacred isle of the *Hierni* rich in turf among the waves
Diodorus Siculus	5.3.3	c. 60–30 B.C.	Cannibals on island of *Iris*
Julius Caesar	*Gallic War* 5.13	c. 54 B.C.	*Hibernia* half the size of Britain
Strabo	*Geography* 1.4.3–5; 2.1.13, 17–18; 2.5.8, 14, 34; 4.5.4	c. A.D. 19	*Ierne* a cold land north of Britain at edge of habitable world, inhabitants are incestuous cannibals
Isidorus	*Geographi Graeci Minores* 2.509	early 1st century A.D.	*Iernē* larger (?) than Britain
Pomponius Mela	*De chorographia* 3.53	c. A.D. 44	Climate of *Iuverna* good for grain and cattle, inhabitants most ignorant of virtue and duty
Pliny	*Natural History* 4.102–3	c. A.D. 77	*Hibernia* oblong in shape
Pseudo-Aristotle	*De mundo* 3.393b	c. 50 B.C.–A.D. 100	*Iernē* larger than Mediterranean islands
Tacitus	*Agricola* 24; *Annals* 12.32	c. A.D. 98, 118	Agricola hoped to invade *Hibernia*, climate and inhabitants similar to Britain, visited by Roman merchants, Irish petty king in Agricola's retinue
Juvenal	*Satire* 2.159–63	c. A.D. 118	Roman might advanced beyond the shores of *Iuverna*
Dionysius Periegetes	*Orbis descriptio* 565–69	early 2d century A.D.	Two *Bretanides* isles largest of all islands
Ptolemy	*Almagest* 2.6.25–27; *Geography* 1.11, 2.1–2, 7.5, 8.3	c. A.D. 150	Position of Little *Bretannia*, merchants report *Iuvernia* twenty-day journey from east to west, capes, rivers, tribes, towns, nearby islands

Source	Citation	Date	Description
Apuleius	*De mundo* 7	c. A.D. 160–70	*Hibernia* larger than Mediterranean islands
Herodian	*De prosodia catholica* 7.175, 11.296, 12.327	c. A.D. 160–80	Forms of *I(u)ern-* as grammatical examples
Solinus	*Collectanea rerum memorabilium* 22.2–6	c. A.D. 200	Inhabitants of *Hibernia* bloody savages, rich agriculture, no snakes or bees
Panegyric on Constantius Caesar	11.4	A.D. 297	Half-naked *Hiberni* and Picts
Maritime Itinerary	508.3–509.1	late 3d century A.D.	Island in *Hiverione* Sea
Panegyric on Constantine Augustus	7.2	A.D. 310	Constantius I not interested in conquering *Hibernia*
Nomina provinciarum omnium	13	c. A.D. 312	*Scoti* tribe increased in number
Orphic Argonautica	1165–66, 1180–81	late 4th century A.D.	*Argo* sails near isle of *Iernē*
Pacatus	*Panegyric on Theodosius* 5.2	c. A.D. 389	*Scoti* driven back to own swamps
Ammianus Marcellinus	*History* 20.1.1, 26.4.5, 27.8.5	c. A.D. 392	Raids of *Scotti* and *Attacotti*
Historia Augusta	*Tacitus* 15.2	late 4th century A.D.	Prophesy of Roman rule of *Iuverna*
Pseudo-Hegesippus	*Jewish War* 5.15b	late 4th/5th century A.D.	*Scotia* fears the Romans
Jerome	*Adversus Jovinianum* 2.7; *Epistle* 69.415; *Epistle* 123.1038; *Commentary on Jeremiah* 1 (prologue), 3 (prologue)	c. A.D. 390–415	Personally witnessed *Atticoti* or *Scoti* cannibalism in Gaul, *Scotti* and *Atticotti* have wives in common, *Scotti* ignorant of Moses and the prophets, stupid *Scottus* critic with porridge-breath
Prudentius	*Apotheosis* 212–16	c. A.D. 390–95	Even half-wild *Scottus* knows a supreme order prevails
Symmachus	*Epistle* 2.77	c. A.D. 393	Seven *Scotti* dogs brought to Rome
Servius	*Commentary on Virgil's Georgics* 1.30	late 4th century A.D.	Thule lies beyond *Hibernia*

Author	Passage(s)	Date	Summary
Claudian	Panegyric on the Third Consulship of Honorius 54–56; Panegyric on the Fourth Consulship of Honorius 8.30–33; Epithalamium to Palladius 88–90; On Stilicho's Consulship 2.247–55; Gothic War 416–18	c. A.D. 396–402	Scotti pursued, Hiverne wept at dead Scotti, Scotti roused all Hiverne, legions protect Britain from Scotti
Marcianus	Periplus of the Outer Sea 1.8, 2 (prologue), 41–44	c. A.D. 400 (?)	Iwernia smaller than Britain and lies to the west, capes, distances, and nearby seas
Stobaeus	Anthologium 1.40.1	early 5th century A.D.	Iernē and Britain larger than other islands
Orosius	Historiae adversum paganos 1.2.75, 80–82	c. A.D. 417	Hibernia inhabited by Scotti, Scenae river, tribes, Scotti on island of Mevania
Pseudo-Agathemerus	Geographia compendaria 4, 8	post–2d century A.D.	Iwernia lies west of Britain, third largest island in the world

The Names of Ireland

Name	Source
insula sacra ("Sacred Island")	Avienus
Iris (Ἶρις)	Diodorus Siculus
Iernē (Ἰέρνη)	Strabo, Isidorus, Pseudo-Aristotle, Herodian, *Orphic Argonautica*, Stobaeus
Iwernia (Ἰουερνία)	Ptolemy, Herodian, Marcianus, Pseudo-Agathemerus
Iuverna	Pomponius Mela, Juvenal, *Historia Augusta*
Hibernia	Caesar, Pliny, Tacitus, Apuleius, Solinus, *Panegyric on Constantine Augustus*, Servius, Orosius
Hiverne	Claudian
Hiverione	*Maritime Itinerary*
Scotia	Pseudo-Hegesippus
Mikra Brettania (Μικρὰ Βρεττανία)	Ptolemy

References

Ahlqvist, A. 1982. *The Early Irish Linguist.* Helsinki: The Finnish Society of Sciences and Letters.

Allen, W. 1978. *Vox Latina.* Cambridge: Cambridge University Press.

Bateson, J. 1973. "Roman Material from Ireland: A Re-Consideration." *Proceedings of the Royal Irish Academy* 73C: 21–97.

———. 1976. "Further Finds of Roman Material from Ireland." *Proceedings of the Royal Irish Academy* 76C: 171–80.

Bergin, O. 1946. "*Ériu* and the Ablaut." *Ériu* 14: 147–53.

Berthelot, A., ed. 1934. *Ora maritima.* Paris: Librairie ancienne honoré champion.

Billy, P. 1993. *Thesaurus Linguae Gallicae.* Hildesheim: Olms-Weidmann.

Bourke, E. 1989. "Stoneyford: A First-Century Roman Burial from Ireland." *Archaeology Ireland* 3.2: 56–57.

Brindley, A., and J. Lanting. 1990. "A Roman Boat in Ireland." *Archaeology Ireland* 4.3: 10–11.

Buck, C. 1955. *The Greek Dialects.* Chicago: University of Chicago Press.

Carney, J. 1975. "The Invention of the Ogam Cipher." *Ériu* 26: 53–65.

Carson, R., and C. O'Kelly. 1977. "A Catalogue of the Roman Coins from Newgrange, Co. Meath and Notes on the Coins and Related Finds." *Proceedings of the Royal Irish Academy* 77C: 35–55.

Charles-Edwards, T., and F. Kelly, eds. 1983. *Bechbretha.* Dublin: Dublin Institute for Advanced Studies.

Cunliffe, B. 1988. *Greeks, Romans and Barbarians.* New York: Methuen.

Cuntz, O. 1929. *Itineraria Romana.* Vol. 1. Leipzig: Teubner.

De Paor, L. 1993. *St. Patrick's World.* Notre Dame, Ind.: University of Notre Dame Press.

Dillon, M. 1977. "The Irish Settlements in Wales." *Celtica* 12: 1–11.

Dittenberger, W. 1915–24. *Sylloge Inscriptionum Graecarum.* Leipzig: Hirzelium.

Duval, P., and G. Pinault. 1988. *Recueil des inscriptions gauloises.* Vol. 3. Paris: Éditions du CNRS.

Elliott, R. 1959. *Runes: An Introduction.* Manchester: Manchester University Press.

Eska, J. 1989. *Towards an Interpretation of the Hispano-Celtic Inscription of Botorrita.* Innsbruck: Institut für Sprachwissenschaft.

Eska, J., and D. Evans. 1993. "Continental Celtic." In *The Celtic Languages,* ed. M. Ball, 26–63. London: Routledge.

Evans, D. 1967. *Gaulish Personal Names.* Oxford: Clarendon.

Freeman, P. 1995. "Greek and Roman Views of Ireland: A Checklist." *Emania* 13: 11–13.

———. 1996. "The Earliest Greek Sources on the Celts." *Études celtiques* 32: 11–48.

Gwynn, E. 1913. *The Metrical Dindshenchas.* Part 3. Dublin: Hodges, Figgis.

Hamp, E. 1953. Review of I. J. Gelb, *A Study of Writing: The Foundations of Grammatology.* In *Zeitschrift für celtische Philologie* 24: 308–12.

Haverfield, F. 1913. "Ancient Rome and Ireland." *English Historical Review* 109: 1–12.

Hawkes, C. 1977. *Pytheas: Europe and the Greek Explorers.* The Eighth Annual J. L. Myres Memorial Lecture. Oxford: Blackwell.

Heiberg, J., ed. *Syntaxis mathematica.* Leipzig: Teubner.

Heneken, H. 1942. "Ballinderry Crannog No. 2." *Proceedings of the Royal Irish Academy* 47: 1–76.

Henry, F. 1953. "A Wooden Hut on Inishkea North, Co. Mayo." *Journal of the Royal Society of Antiquaries of Ireland* 83: 163–78.

Holtz, L. 1981. *Donat.* Paris: Éditions du CNRS.

Jackson, K. 1953. *Language and History in Early Britain.* Cambridge, Mass.: Harvard University Press.

———. 1954. "The Pictish Language." In *The Problem of the Picts.* Westport, Conn.: Greenwood.

Jackson, R. 1990. "A New Collyrium Stamp from Cambridge and a Corrected Reading of the Stamp from Caistor-by-Norwich." *Britannia* 21: 275–83.

Kaster, R. 1988. *Guardians of Language.* Berkeley: University of California Press.

Kenney, J. 1929. *The Sources for the Early History of Ireland.* Vol. 1. New York: Columbia University Press.

Killeen, J. 1976. "Ireland in the Greek and Roman Writers." *Proceedings of the Royal Irish Academy* 76C: 207–15.

Koch, J. 1991. "Ériu, Alba, and Letha: When Was a Language Ancestral to Gaelic First Spoken in Ireland?" *Emania* 9: 17–27.

———. 1995. "The Conversion and the Transition from Primitive to Old Irish *c.* 367–*c.* 637." *Emania* 13: 39–50.

Koch, J., and J. Carey. 1995. *The Celtic Heroic Age.* Andover, Mass.: Celtic Studies Publications.

Kurylowicz, J. 1961. "Note sur l'ogam." *Bulletin de la société de linguistique* 56: 1–5.

Lambert, P. 1994. *La langue gauloise.* Paris: Éditions Errance.

Lejeune, M. 1955. *Celtiberica.* Salamanca: Ediciones Universidad de Salamanca.

———. 1971. *Lepontica.* Paris: Société d'éditions les belles lettres.

———. 1985a. *Le plomb magique du Larzac et les sorcières gauloises.* Paris: Éditions du CNRS.

———. 1985b. *Recueil des inscriptions gauloises.* Vol. 1. Paris: Éditions du CNRS.

———. 1988. *Recueil des inscriptions gauloises.* Vol. 2.1. Paris: Éditions du CNRS.

Lentz, A., ed. 1867. *Herodiani Technici Reliqiae.* Leipzig: Teubner.

Lloyd-Morgan, G. 1976. "A Note on Some Celtic Discs from Ireland and the Province of Lower Germany." *Proceedings of the Royal Irish Academy* 76C: 217–22.

Lorimer, W., ed. 1933. *Aristotelis qui fertur libellus de mundo.* Paris: Les belles lettres.

Lynn, C. 1986. "Navan Fort." *Emania* 1: 11–19.

Mac Cana, P. 1985. *Celtic Mythology.* New York: Peter Bedrick.

McManus, D. 1983. "A Chronology of the Latin Loan-Words in Early Irish." *Ériu* 34: 21–71.

———. 1991. *A Guide to Ogam.* Maynooth: An Sagart.

MacNeill, E. 1919. *Phases of Irish History.* Dublin: Gill and Son.

Mac White, E. 1961. "Contributions to a Study of Ogam Memorial Stones." *Zeitschrift für celtische Philologie* 28: 294–308.

Mallory, J., and T. McNeill. 1991. *The Archaeology of Ulster.* Belfast: Institute of Irish Studies.

Mattingly, H., and J. Pearce. 1937. "The Coleraine Hoard." *Antiquity* 2: 39–45.

Meid, W. 1992. *Gaulish Inscriptions.* Budapest: Hungarian Academy of Sciences.

Mommsen, T. 1895. *C. Iulius Solini Collectanea rerum memorabilium.* Berlin: Weidmann.

Müller, K., ed. 1855. *Geographi Graeci Minores.* 2 vols. Paris: Didot.

———. 1883. *Claudii Ptolemaei geographia.* Paris: Didot.

Murphy, J., ed. 1977. *Ora maritima.* Chicago: Ares.

Mynors, R. 1964. *XII Panegyrici Latini.* Oxford: Clarendon.

Nash, D. 1976. "Reconstructing Poseidonios' Celtic Ethnography: Some Considerations." *Britannia* 7: 111–26.

Nobbe, C., ed. 1843. *Claudii Ptolemaei geographia.* Leipzig: Teubner.

Ó Cathasaigh, T. 1984. "The Déisi and Dyfed." *Éigse* 20: 1–33.

Ó Cuív, B. 1983. *The Linguistic Training of the Mediaeval Irish Poet.* Dublin: Dublin Institute for Advanced Studies.

Ogilvie, R., and I. Richmond. 1967. *Cornelii Taciti De vita Agricola.* Oxford: Clarendon.

O'Rahilly, T. 1946a. "On the Origin of the Names *Érainn* and *Ériu.*" *Ériu* 14: 7–28.

———. 1946b. *Early Irish History and Mythology.* Dublin: Dublin Institute for Advanced Studies.

Ó Ríordáin, S. 1947. "Roman Material in Ireland." *Proceedings of the Royal Irish Academy* 51C: 35–82.

Orpen, G. 1894. "Ptolemy's Map of Ireland." *Journal of the Royal Society of Antiquaries of Ireland* 24: 115–28.

Piggott, S. 1953. "Bronze Double-Axes in the British Isles." *Proceedings of the Prehistoric Society* 19: 224–26.

Pokorny, J. 1953. "Die Geographie Irlands bei Ptolemaios." *Zeitschrift für Celtische Philologie* 24: 94–120.

Raftery, B. 1994. *Pagan Celtic Ireland*. London: Thames and Hudson.

———. 1996. "Drumanagh and Roman Ireland." *Archaeology Ireland* 10.1: 17–19.

Raftery, J. 1959. "A Travelling-Man's Gear of Christian Times." *Proceedings of the Royal Irish Academy* 60C: 1–8.

Rhys, J. 1882. *Celtic Britain*. London: Society for Promoting Christian Knowledge.

Riese, A. 1878. *Geographi Latini Minores*. Heilbronnae: Apud Henningeros Fratres.

Rivet, A., and C. Smith. 1979. *The Place-Names of Roman Britain*. Princeton: Princeton University Press.

Rynne, E. 1976. "The La Tène and Roman Finds from Lambay, County Dublin: A Re-assessment." *Proceedings of the Royal Irish Academy* 76C: 231–44.

Shetelig, H. 1949. "Roman Coins Found in Iceland." *Antiquity* 91: 161–63.

Sihler, A. 1995. *New Comparative Grammar of Greek and Latin*. Oxford: Oxford University Press.

Stevenson, E., ed. 1932. *The Geography*. New York: New York Public Library. Reprint 1991, New York: Dover.

Stevenson, J. 1989. "The Beginnings of Literacy in Ireland." *Proceedings of the Royal Irish Academy* 89C: 127–65.

Stichtenoth, D., ed. 1968. *Ora maritima*. Darmstadt: Wissenschaftliche Buchgesellschaft.

Stone, J., and L. Thomas. 1956. "The Use and Distribution of Faience in the Ancient East and Prehistoric Europe." *Proceedings of the Prehistoric Society* 22: 37–84.

Thurneysen, R. 1937. "Zum Ogom." *Beiträge zur Geschichte der deutschen Sprache und Literatur* 61: 188–208.

———. 1980. *A Grammar of Old Irish*. Dublin: Dublin Institute for Advanced Studies.

Tierney, J. 1959. "Ptolemy's Map of Scotland." *Journal of Hellenic Studies* 79: 132–48.

———. 1960. "The Celtic Ethnography of Posidonius." *Proceedings of the Royal Irish Academy* 60C: 189–275.

———. 1976. "The Greek Geographic Tradition and Ptolemy's Evidence for Irish Geography." *Proceedings of the Royal Irish Academy* 76C: 257–65.

Tomlin, R. 1987. "Was Ancient British Celtic Ever a Written Language?" *Bulletin of the Board of Celtic Studies* 34: 18–25.

Vendryes, J. 1948. "L'écriture ogamique et ses origines." *Études celtiques* 4: 83–116.

———. 1987. *Lexique étymologique de l'irlandais ancien "C"*. Dublin: Dublin Institute for Advanced Studies.

Vian, F., ed. 1987. *Les argonautiques orphiques*. Paris: Société d'édition des belles lettres.

Wachsmuth, C., ed. 1884. *Ioannis Stobaei Anthologii*. Berlin: Weidmann.

Warner, R. 1976. "Some Observations on the Context and Importation of Exotic Material in Ireland, from the First Century B.C. to the Second Century A.D." *Proceedings of the Royal Irish Academy* 76C: 267–92.

———. 1995. "Tuathal Techtmar: A Myth or Ancient Literary Evidence for a Roman Invasion?" *Emania* 13: 23–32.

Weisgerber, L. 1931. "Galatische Sprachreste." In *Natalicium Johannes Geffcken zum 70. Geburtstag*, 151–75. Heidelberg: Carl Winters.

Index

Page numbers in bold indicate references to maps.